W9-CFW-257

BE YOUR
BEST
YOU

BE STRONG!

A HERO'S GUIDE
TO BEING RESILIENT

ELSIE OLSON

Consulting Editor, Diane Craig, M.A./Reading Specialist

Super Sandcastle

An Imprint of Abdo Publishing
abdobooks.com

abdobooks.com

Published by Abdo Publishing, a division of ABDO, PO Box 398166, Minneapolis, Minnesota 55439. Copyright © 2020 by Abdo Consulting Group, Inc. International copyrights reserved in all countries. No part of this book may be reproduced in any form without written permission from the publisher. Super SandCastle™ is a trademark and logo of Abdo Publishing.

Printed in the United States of America, North Mankato, Minnesota
052019
092019

THIS BOOK CONTAINS
RECYCLED MATERIALS

Design: Sarah DeYoung, Mighty Media, Inc.
Production: Mighty Media, Inc.
Editor: Jessica Rusick
Cover Photographs: iStockphoto; Shutterstock Images
Interior Photographs: iStockphoto; Mighty Media, Inc.; Shutterstock Images

Library of Congress Control Number: 2018966952

Publisher's Cataloging-in-Publication Data
Names: Olson, Elsie, author.
Title: Be strong!: a hero's guide to being resilient / by Elsie Olson
Other title: A hero's guide to being resilient
Description: Minneapolis, Minnesota : Abdo Publishing, 2020 | Series: Be your best you
Identifiers: ISBN 9781532119682 (lib. bdg.) | ISBN 9781532174445 (ebook)
Subjects: LCSH: Resilience (Personality trait)--Juvenile literature. | Adaptive behavior--Juvenile literature.
    | Hardiness--Juvenile literature. | Toughness (Personality trait)--Juvenile literature. | Heroism--
    Juvenile literature. | Self-confidence in children--Juvenile literature.
Classification: DDC 158.1--dc23

Super SandCastle™ books are created by a team of professional educators, reading specialists, and content developers around five essential components—phonemic awareness, phonics, vocabulary, text comprehension, and fluency—to assist young readers as they develop reading skills and strategies and increase their general knowledge. All books are written, reviewed, and leveled for guided reading, early reading intervention, and Accelerated Reader™ programs for use in shared, guided, and independent reading and writing activities to support a balanced approach to literacy instruction.

CONTENTS

BE YOUR BEST YOU!

Have you ever tried to learn something new? But when it was hard, you felt a bit blue?

Superheroes stay strong when tasks are tough. They keep trying, even when things are rough.

YOU HAVE THE POWER.
BE A HERO TOO.
BE STRONG AND **RESILIENT**.

BE YOUR BEST
YOU!

WHAT IS RESILIENCE?

Resilience means being able to handle tough situations. Resilient kids have strong minds. They make mistakes. They go through hard things. They feel sad sometimes. But they always keep trying.

Are You **Resilient**?

- Do you try new foods, even if you are not sure you will like them?

- Do you keep playing a game, even if you are losing?

- Do you talk to an adult if you are feeling sad?

These are signs of resilience!

STRONG MIND, AMAZING YOU!

A strong mind is an **amazing** tool. It can help you be successful at lots of things. But no one is good at everything. And that's okay!

TAKE A LITTLE RISK

Superheroes aren't afraid to take some chances. This can be scary. But taking healthy risks makes you stronger and smarter. You don't know what you can do until you try!

BE HEROIC AND BE SMART!

Heroes don't take risks that put themselves or others in danger.

11

PERSEVERANCE

Heroes have **perseverance**. This means they don't give up. They make a goal and stick to it.

Choose a goal you want to stick to. It might be hard at first. That's okay! Keep practicing until you get better.

DRAW A DREAM BOARD

Resilience is easier if you know what you are working toward. Draw pictures of your goal. Try to keep it **realistic** for a first step.

After you reach your goal, set a harder one!

SUPERPOWER!
PROBLEM-SOLVE

Sometimes heroes get stuck. And so will you. That means it's time to use one of your brain's best superpowers. These are your problem-solving skills!

PROBLEM-SOLVING 101

Stuck? Try these simple steps!

BREAK A TOUGH TASK INTO SMALLER STEPS.

FIGURE OUT THE HARDEST STEP.

BRAINSTORM THREE DIFFERENT <u>SOLUTIONS</u>.

TEST ONE SOLUTION. IF IT DOESN'T WORK, TRY ANOTHER ONE!

TALK ABOUT YOUR FEELINGS

Resilient kids still feel sad and mad. But you can be a hero when you feel blue.

Share your feelings with a trusted adult. That's the first step to feeling better!

BE HELPFUL, NOT HELPLESS

Doing something kind can make you feel better when you are sad. Offer to help your parents with a chore. Or read your brother or sister a story.

LEARN FROM YOUR MISTAKES

Everyone makes mistakes, even heroes! But mistakes can teach you a lot. Think about what you can do differently next time.

REMEMBER TO **APOLOGIZE**

IF YOUR MISTAKE HURT SOMEONE'S FEELINGS.

Treat others how you want to be treated!

BE POSITIVE

Self-talk is the way you talk about yourself. Make positive self-talk your superpower. Turn **negative** thoughts around by adding something positive! This can give you the strength to stick to a tough task.

20

NEGATIVE

I am always the slowest
soccer player.

I can't spell.

POSITIVE

I'm not as fast as other
kids on my team. But I'm a
good teammate!

Spelling is hard for me.
But I can get better
with practice!

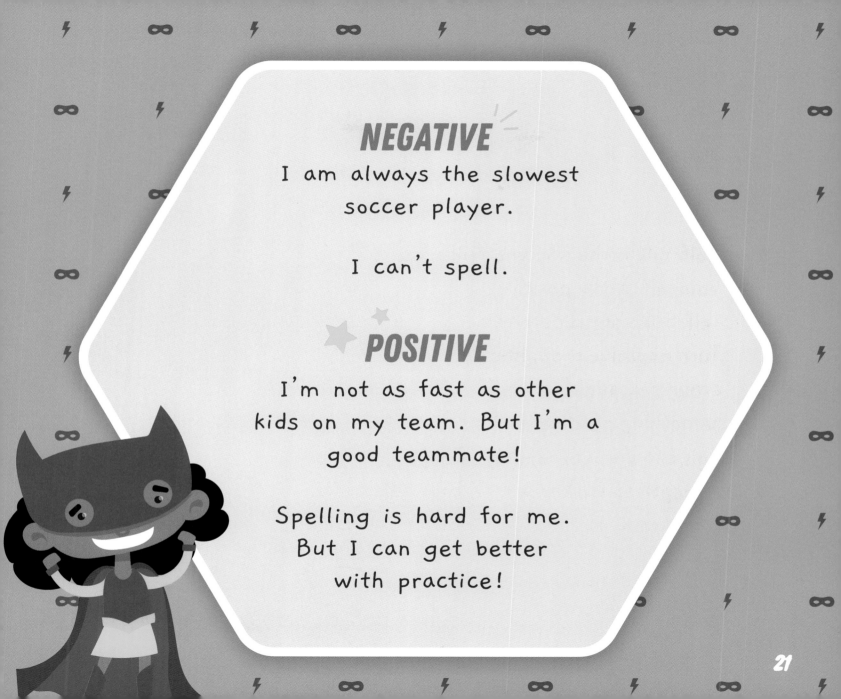

BE A HERO!

It's your turn to take a stand.
Act like a hero. Lend a hand.

With the words you say and
the things you do, be
strong and **resilient**.
Be your best you!

WHAT WOULD YOU DO?

Being a hero is about making strong and **resilient** choices. How would you use your superpowers in the situations below?

You get a bad grade on a quiz you studied hard for.

Your soccer team loses a game.

Someone says something mean to you and hurts your feelings.

GLOSSARY

amazing – wonderful or surprising.

apologize – to say that you are sorry about something.

negative – bad or hurtful.

perseverance – the quality that allows a person to keep trying to do something even though it is difficult.

realistic – showing things as they are or could be in real life.

resilient – able to become strong or healthy again after something bad happens. Someone who is resilient shows resilience.

solution – a way of solving a problem.

ONLINE RESOURCES

Booklinks
NONFICTION NETWORK
FREE! ONLINE NONFICTION RESOURCES

To learn more about being strong and resilient, visit **abdobooklinks.com** or scan this QR code. These links are routinely monitored and updated to provide the most current information available.

24

"My father had just passed away at age 94 when I was introduced to *Sunrises and Sunsets*. Holley Kelley's honest voice reached out to me in every chapter of this informative and inspiring book about preparing for the end of life's journey."

~ Andrea C. Birch, Ph.D., Dean, College of Fine Arts and Humanities
Professor of Philosophy, Brenau University

"Working on this book with Holley has been FUN, rewarding, and a life-enriching experience for me. Holley is the real deal. She is flexible, dedicated to making this book the best it possibly can be, and is tireless in its production. I can hardly wait until the book is actually in print so I can gather a few of my friends together, start a group, and work the process together. I anticipate not only a very supportive, meaningful connection but one that will make it FUN and act as a cure for any tendencies to procrastinate. Who knows?! As a former therapist, I may end up leading several groups! This book definitely has the makings for a profound and practical outcome. I can't think of a better gift to leave my loved ones than the completion of this book and all its suggestions."

~ Cleone Reed, MSE, Graphic Designer,
Editor, and Production Manager, Robert D. Reed Publishers

"Sometimes in life you come across something that you never knew you were missing until you find it. This book is just one of those things.

"We all know that we have to plan for the end of our lives, and this is the first and only comprehensive guide I have found to help with that important planning.

"This is a must-have item to take stock of your own life at any age and help not only yourself but those you must inevitably leave behind.

"*Sunrises and Sunsets* will be an indispensable tool in my gerontology professional toolbox and in my own personal life."

~ Ginger Ragans, MS, C.P.G., CAPS

"What a GREAT book this is! So many people fail to prepare for their final sunset! *Sunrises and Sunsets* will help anyone overcome that obstacle! Holley's informative work sheets are easy to follow and this book is an enjoyable process from beginning to end! We have completed many of the suggestions in this book, and the ones overlooked are now underway! We will undoubtedly be recommending this book to all of our friends and relatives! Thank you for informing us of this unique and wonderful book so we can share it with others!"

~ Bob and Cynthia DeTorres

"Having recently become a new mother mere days after losing my father-in-law, I have come to fully understand the profound nature of this book. Holley Kelley's work not only demystifies the process for preparing for our own 'final sunset,' it does so while offering a beautiful and meaningful celebration of life."

~ Leslie Hodges, B.A., M.A.

"Through her narrative discussions, checklists, and practical approach, Holley Kelley helps us navigate end-of-life issues in a way that simply works! *Sunrises and Sunsets* helps define and plan our final journey, in a gentle and entertaining format. She is both an instructive and valued guide for anyone who wishes to get their affairs in order!"

~ Gary Gartner, CEO, SpaceFlight Memorial Systems

"In our quiet moments each one of us know we aren't going to escape death, but that doesn't stop us from trying! As a pastor I see up close the anxiety, the grief, and the loss that often accompanies our final days on earth. Yet sometimes I get to see something else: a life that has intentionally created a gracious space to die well.

"Fortunately Holley Kelley has created a marvelous resource that can help you and those whom you love have thoughtful honest conversation about how to live and die well. This book is a workbook—a way of collecting and assembling important information, and providing a way of having the kind of conversation where our deepest hopes are expressed and our greatest longings shared. This workbook belongs in the hands of the young and the old. In short, all of us who want to live well."

~ Rev. Laura Sumner Truax, Senior Pastor, LaSalle Street Church
Author, *Undone: When Coming Apart Puts You Back Together*, Intervarsity Press, 2013

"With more 'senior citizens' alive on the planet than at any other time, greater percentages of those of us who are of age to qualify for membership in that group have a life expectancy far exceeding that of our parents and grandparents. In my own experience, I have outlived my father by 20 years and my mother by a decade. As a group we do see the end of life as a part of life. Yet, many times we are no more prepared for this inevitability than our parents were. It is not that we mind so much thinking about moving on as it is that we don't really know how to think about it. Holley Kelley has provided us with an amazing guidebook that is both sensible and sensitive to help us with our departure and journey, easing the anxiety and fear with simplicity and demystification."

~ David Morrison, Director of Communications & Publications, Brenau University

"Holley Kelley's book addresses what remains after we are gone...our legacies! Whether we are aware of it or not, we create our legacies by the way we live and what we do each day of our lives. *Sunrises and Sunsets* is a great tool for those who choose to plan for their Final Sunset, as well as articulate their legacies with and on purpose. This do-it-yourself guide book is a must for all who want to leave a clear picture of who they are, as well as what they want, for those they care about and for generations to follow."

~ James F. (Buddy) Thomas, Jr. – Founder Chie Planning Officer, Superior Planning, Inc., providing
Multi-Generational Family Wealth and Relationship Management assistance since 1982,
Author of *The Coming Widow Boom*

"Holley Kelley provides clear, logical guidelines for getting one's affairs in order while there is still time. Her lively writing style, wit, verve, and generosity of spirit make the process a surprising adventure."

~ Dr. Nan Morrison, Emeritus Professor of English, College of Charleston

"For many of us, planning our own death is never easy and often avoided; but in a delightful and engaging way, Holley Kelley shows how planning for death enables us to live more fully. Her fresh perspective has produced a one-of-a-kind book that provides plenty of practical advice while also encouraging us to document our legacy and ensure our desires are heard and fulfilled. I will advise all of my clients and friends to get a copy of this book and use it throughout the years. You, and the people you love, will be glad you did!"

~ Linda Sumner Weinberg, Attorney

SUNRISES AND SUNSETS

Final Affairs Forged with Flair, Finesse, and **FUN**ctionality

By Gerontologist and Journalist

Holley Kelley, M.S., C.P.G.

Foreword by Dr. Bonnie J. Kin

ROBERT D. REED PUBLISHERS

Robert D. Reed Publishers
P.O. Box 1992
Bandon, OR 97411
Phone: 541-347-9882; Fax: -9883
E-mail: 4bobreed@msn.com
Website: www.rdrpublishers.com

Cover Designer and Editor: Cleone Reed
Book Designer: Susan Leonard

Photos and Artwork: many obtained from the public domain off of the Internet; some from the author's and editor's private collections, and others personally created by Cleone Reed

All definitions in the book from http://dictionary.reference.com

ISBN 13: 978-1-934759-97-4
ISBN 10: 1-934759-97-X

Library of Congress Number: 2015946123

Designed and Formatted in the United States of America; printed in China

Disclaimer for *Sunrises and Sunsets* book:

Although the author, publisher, and copyright owner have made every effort to ensure that the information in this book was correct at press time, the author, publisher, and copyright owner do not assume and hereby disclaim any liability to any party for any loss, damage, or disruption caused by errors or omissions, whether such errors or omissions result from negligence, accident, or any other cause. External links for third party websites are provided as a service to users; and the author, publishers, and copyright owner do not accept any responsibility or liability for the accuracy or content of those sites.

There is no express or implied warranty on behalf of the author, publisher, or copyright owner; and they accept no liability or responsibility for any errors or omissions for the information, nor do they accept any liability for damages as a result of the material contained herein.

Some identifying details have been changed to protect the privacy of individuals. This book contains information from the author's educational experiences, professional background, research, and personal encounters. While every effort has been made to ensure accuracy and validity of the information provided, the author, publisher and copyright owner disclaim any personal or collective liability, either directly or indirectly, as a result of utilization of the materials, information, and guidance offered in this book and furthermore, accept no responsibility or liability for errors, inaccuracies, omissions, or inconsistencies. This book is intended to be utilized as a general reference guide. It is not intended as a substitute for advice of physicians, attorneys, financial planners, or other qualified professionals. The reader should consult professionals in matters relating to his or her specific circumstances with respect to any specific questions or situations that may need attention.

For my mother,
who has shown me limitless strength,
courage and passion for life.
You are my inspiration.

It is good to have an end to journey toward;
but it is the journey that matters, in the end.
~Ernest Hemingway

ACKNOWLEDGMENTS

There was no other place for this book to land, but on the desk, and in the honest hearts and capable hands of Bob and Cleone Reed, namely Robert D. Reed Publishers. It has been a pleasurable journey working with both of you, but, especially you, Cleone, as we worked so closely together for so long. We made a great team, working out the details, to make this book something truly unique. I am proud of our work, as this book has become a special memento that people can use, enjoy, and cherish as they forge their plans for latter-life planning. You are truly beautiful people whom I treasure. And I can think of no other place for *Sunrises and Sunsets* to be, so for both of you, I am grateful.

Dr. Bonnie Kin, your expertise in the area of Geropsychology, Gerontology, Alzheimer's disease, Health Psychology, Attachment, and Eating Disorders, is extraordinary. As a gerontologist, I am honored and privileged for the opportunity to have mentored and studied under your professional guidance and expertise at Brenau University. When I shared my desire to forge this project, your faith in me as a student and a professional was encouraging and inspiring. And, when you received it, you immediately let me know I must publish it. Thank you for urging me to not allow this project to go dormant. And, also for convincing me that I had created something that fulfilled a positive need for the greater good, service, and benefit to society. Now, instead of sitting on a shelf, collecting dust, it is being unveiled for the world to read, enjoy, and most importantly utilize. For that, and you, I am eternally grateful.

Attorney Linda Weinberg, thank you for your early reviews of the book, and convincing me that *Sunrises and Sunsets* had a platform and could benefit society. Your expertise and professional background were invaluable. You have been unbelievably supportive of my efforts. You are one of the kindest and most benevolent people I have never met. Your many contributions are forever cherished and appreciated.

Dr. Andrea Birch, I was on the fence when I received your letter about the book. I always say, "Humpty Dumpty didn't fall; he was pushed!" In that moment, I knew what I needed to do. That was the "push" I needed, and in that moment I knew I must explore publishing venues. Your letter showed me what a positive impact this book could have in the lives of others, and it was also my path of enlightenment!

Dr. Nan Morrison, I am so grateful for your honest and deliberate review of the book. The insight and feedback you provided assured me that publishing this book was the right decision and there was an audience eager to receive it. You are not only delightful and talented, but also humble and generous. I appreciate your support and confidence in me as a writer. It is my privilege and honor to know you.

Leslie Hodges, B.A., M.A., you were the first to see this book, and I anxiously awaited your insightful feedback. Your well-informed review was great and supportive of which I was happy! You are intelligent and lovely, and your early contributions were fundamentally essential. For that, and you, I am grateful.

I would like to thank and acknowledge my family for their constant support always, and during this process. To my mother, you are not only amazing but also the strongest, most incredible woman I will ever know. My papa, while I was not born to you, you are my father of the heart, and I admire and love you. My children, you are the loves of my life, and are all that I have hoped and dreamed! My husband, thank you for always believing in me, and lovingly supporting my interests and hobbies! My brother, whom I love dearly, you bring out my deepest laughter, and encourage my most spirited side of living, of which only you are capable. My favorite uncle Rick, and you would be, even if I had a hundred—I love our jokes, our laughter, but most of all you. To Jeffrey, whom I truly appreciate, always; Timothy, you are my brother of the soul. And, to my best friend, Kristen—you define friendship.

TABLE OF CONTENTS

SECTION 3—NOTHING LEFT UNSAID—LOVE, LIVE, CELEBRATE!

FOREWORD

Death is the final frontier and something for which most of us are ill prepared. Elisabeth Kübler-Ross said it best when she stated, "Death is the final stage of growth." In my 35 years of working with dying patients and their families, as well as teaching classes in death and dying, I have always thought a "how to" book would be beneficial. It would have been so helpful to my patients and their families and an important teaching tool in classes on death and dying as well as adult development. We have books and manuals on how to prepare for childbirth and how to parent, but there was nothing on how to prepare for death.

Then along came Holley Kelley. It's rare that one comes across someone with the insight and talent that Holley possesses. From the very first day I met Holley in class, I knew she was destined to do something important in the field of death and dying. She did not disappoint. Holley demonstrated an uncanny ability to take a taboo subject and developed a step-by-step way of helping people prepare for end-of-life issues in a warm, compassionate, empathic manner.

Sunrises and Sunsets is a compelling book that provides powerful and practical information on approaching death and dying as well as life and living. Holley has developed a way of approaching and preparing for life's final stages in a comprehensive yet caring way. She does this in a non-threatening, gentle manner and even includes a bit of humor.

The information contained in this book is groundbreaking—finally someone has let death and dying out of the closet and into the mainstream. Finally, someone is willing to discuss it in an open, straightforward manner. From the introduction to the last chapter, this book is chock full of practical, important information presented in a straight-forward way that will appeal to everyone. Indeed, it will help people prepare for their final stage of growth.

This book belongs in everyone's home. Give it as a gift for birthdays, anniversaries, Christmas, Hanukah. Will the recipients initially be offended? Perhaps. However, I guarantee that once they begin reading this book, they will be absorbed in the content and will ultimately write you a very fine thank you note.

I just cannot say enough positive things about Holley and *Sunrises and Sunsets*. She recognized and seized an opportunity to fulfill a much needed niche and she ran with it. I am honored, proud, and humbled that she was my graduate student. I predict this will be a best seller.

Dr. Bonnie J. Kin
Director, M.S. Applied Gerontology
Professor, Psychology
Brenau University, Gainesville, GA

SECTION 1
THE SUN RISES AND THE SUN SETS

PREFACE
About YOUR Book

As sure as the sun peacefully rises each morning and sets beautifully every evening, we too will each face our ultimate destiny. And, in between the sunrises and the sunsets, there's a whole lot of living to be enjoyed!

That is what YOUR book is about: planning for the final sunset, while appreciating all the sunrises in the process. Planning is important in any task or project. We plan all kinds of things in life. But, there's one thing in life that most of us don't really want to plan—our own departure.

While failing to plan is understandable, it makes little sense. Your farewell is your final event. It is a celebration of YOUR life—the one YOU lived and the one YOU made. Your exit should be as amazingly special and unique as you. This is not a time for a cookie-cutter, one-size-fits-all approach. This is a time to show the world who you really are—what matters to you, your proudest moments, who you loved and why.

This is YOUR book. These are YOUR thoughts, wishes, and details about YOUR life. This book is a road map for those left behind to allow them to transition their way through the harsh realities of your departure. It will make life easier on those you love; and they will go through this book, YOUR book, page by page with appreciation of your work, consideration, and efforts.

They will cherish the contents you have left for them. Tears will be shed. Smiles will be born. Love will fill them as they embark on the writings and entries you have so kindly and tenderly created and provided. This book is your gift to them, your final present when you could not be "present" to help them. However, you will be there. This book will take on your life, your heart-felt moments, and your essence.

In fact, it may only be read by you, until that fateful day that it will benefit others to peruse its contents as a means to navigate their way through the wishes and information you have so kindly provided them. Not only is this book a means to establish your current thoughts as they relate to living forward, but it will also help you gain more peace about that inevitable final sunset that we all eventually experience.

This book is a call to action to get all of your affairs in order and remove this burden from those you love. But most of all, it is a time to spread your love, convey your thoughts, and share what you have learned along the way in this amazing journey we call LIFE!

Live life in a spirit of personal gratitude.
It is easy to concern ourselves with the gifts others are receiving.
But, in doing so, we are so preoccupied and distracted
that we never even look down and see the
beautiful present placed directly in front of us.
~HOLLEY KELLEY

How to Use This Book

Some people are story tellers. Some people are challenged to find the right words for nearly any occasion. Either way, this book is a chance for you to free your inner writer. Set your thoughts, feelings, and emotions free as you go through this workbook and make personal entries. There are also pages of the "important" stuff, referred to as your business matters; and by completing these areas, you will save your loved ones a lot of time and frustration. So please take your time on these pages and fill in the information in as detailed a fashion as possible. These matters are very important, as they will help you ensure that your business is handled expeditiously upon your passing.

This book will also ask you to consider matters relating to your personal desires in the event you become incapacitated. These are important considerations, and you will need to think deeply about your answers regarding these difficult circumstances that you may or may not ever face. But, in doing so, at least the work is done, and the choices have been made. Most importantly, they have been made by YOU. The burden of this has not been left up to others where question, guilt, and turmoil could prevail. You have done the arduous work that others should not be burdened with, and they will greatly appreciate that in the end.

> The fear of death
> follows from
> the fear of life.
> A man who lives fully
> is prepared to die
> at any time.
> ~MARK TWAIN

Regarding personal workbook pages, these will take time for you to complete. This book is a work in progress. You cannot expect to complete this in a day or even a week. This is a project that will be ongoing until you have a product in the end that brings you peace and contentment. Until then, it is not final. This book will give you great satisfaction, both while you are working on it, and when it is finished. It is like a wonderful secret or surprise that you are wrapping up to give as a special token of your love and appreciation to those who make life special. This book will be a wonderful addition to your legacy.

The best advice I can give you about using and completing this book is to tackle the sections in any order your mood inspires. While this book is outlined in detail, some days may not be the ideal time for you to write out your own obituary. Perhaps those days would be better for considering business matters and responding to the questionnaires about insurance coverage. But when the mood is right for personal depth and reflection, those are the days to let your words flow from your heart and explore the more personal aspects of YOUR book. In other words, trust your feelings and work on this book accordingly. By doing so, in the end, you will have something that reflects the greatest depth of YOU and conveys your most meaningful and special feelings to those you love.

Getting Organized

To address the functionality of this endeavor, some material that will be generated as a result of working your way through this book will need to be organized separately because of the private and personal material it contains. If you are a reasonably organized person, I encourage you to blaze your own trail of systematic execution as you see fit. For those of you who would prefer some guidance, my suggestion for doing so is to create a notebook or binder with tabbed dividers; or an even more simplistic approach is to use an accordion file. But some of the following materials will also suffice just fine:

~1 - 3-ring binder (clear front sleeve for cover insert works well)

~Tabbed dividers (with 3 ring holes)

~Pocket inserts (with 3 ring holes)

~ OR an according style file folder of your choice

You will assemble the 3-ring binder to prepare for your various inserts as a result of completing this book. Your cover can read, "IMPORTANT MATTERS" or whatever you want to call it. In any respect, you will then begin to label your tabbed divider sections accordingly: "Will," "Advance Directives," "Letters to Loved Ones," "Obituary," etcetera. Then, behind each labeled tabbed divider, you will place pockets. Later, these pockets will be filled with all of your many accomplishments we will complete herein. As for the accordion file, you will simply label the sections and place the contents in each designated slot. In doing so, important documents will be kept organized, yet accessible when needed. Since confidentiality of this material is paramount, if you plan to keep this book in your fire or safe box, be sure to choose a system that will fit.

You can do this all at once or add a section to your binder as you accomplish a new task in this book. Regardless of which method you decide to use, I encourage you to get these supplies ahead of time so that you are organized from the get go. After all, this book is about getting your affairs in order. I want to be sure you have all the tools in place to complete the work book so your papers are not in disarray and can be located when they are needed.

Also, please note in Chapter 19, Checklists, you will find a useful tool to keep you on task. As you complete each item in this book, be sure you go to the checklist and mark that item off accordingly. Additionally, there is also a list I have termed, "Survivor's Checklist." This is checklist that I have included in this book specifically for your survivors. This list will help navigate them through the many necessary and fundamental plans and wishes that you have so deliberately and kindly mapped out for them.

Also, please visit www.sunrisesandsunsetsbook.com for organizational tips, useful information and ideas, as well as accessing additional forms, links, and websites mentioned in this book, some of which is exclusive for readers. You may also share your stories and sunrises and sunsets photos there too, subscribe to my newsletter, see what I am sharing, learn about companies or products I want you to know more about, schedule a *Sunrises and Sunsets* workshop for your group, and much more! I hope you will visit!

And, finally, many of you will have already completed some facets of your advance-care planning. In these circumstances, you have already taken action in some important areas of your life. Even so, this book will further complement and enrich your planning endeavors already in place. This book—though it does not necessarily replace the need for an attorney or financial advisor or related professional—certainly works well in conjunction with professional counsel and lends incredible personal depth to your plans and ultimately your legacy.

So, either way, this book will take you well beyond paperwork, decisions, and legalities. This book will encourage you to delve deep into the true essence of your life experiences and emotions and inspire you to live each day with fewer burdens and more joy and enrichment.

What's Inside?

While I have worked to keep this simple, that is not to say completing it is easy. There is A LOT of stuff in here! But, I assure you that if you take your time and engage in the process, you will truly enjoy some of your planning exercises. There are a couple of important clarifications, moving forward. Most of what is covered in this book is intended for a general audience. Unique and extenuating circumstances may require further professional guidance or research beyond these pages.

Also, you will notice I use the term "those you care about," "family," and "loved ones" a lot in this book. That is because I feel that family can be more than a genetically-tethered gene pool of similar DNA, traits, and characteristics. Your family may include those people who have sustained and endured the test of time and those who have provided support and unwavering love and devotion to you. They do not even have to be someone you have known your entire life. They just have to be those individuals that you call "your people."

You must remember, family is often born of blood,

but it does not depend on blood.

Nor is it exclusive of friendship.

Family members can be your best friends, you know.

And best friends, whether or not they are related to you,

can be your family.

~TRENTON LEE STEWARD

The Mysterious Benedict Society

Inside this book you will find a place that you can go to express the wonderful love you want to leave for those you care about to read when they need to feel it most. We don't just dive into the details of your final wishes like checking off a grocery list. We explore this notion slowly. We get there together, but you are the "final" author of this book. We consider some thought-provoking questions that not only help you understand your state of living today but also may help you to gain peace about your eventual death.

Most people will begin their journey not knowing what their final wishes are and what they wish to convey to others. If you begin with a blank slate with no concrete ideas, that is fine. This book, like life, is a journey into the great unknown. Your personal thoughts and considerations may evolve and change several times as we move through the sections together.

You may not know your point of view on difficult decisions, such as whether you want to be buried or cremated. But in this book you have the opportunity to consider both and to take your time deciding. You may not know what is on your bucket list, mainly because you don't even have a bucket list. This book may inspire you to begin creating one. Whether you have months of life remaining or several decades, all the material herein applies just the same. The answers may be different, but then again, so are you!

No matter what age you are,

or what your circumstances might be,

you are special, and you still have something unique to offer.

Your life, because of who you are, has meaning.

~BARBARA DE ANGELIS

Inside this book you will record all the details of your business and personal life, so that your specific matters can be handled with ease. These pages allow you to share things that you may have never revealed before, mainly because the questions may have never been posed. The readers of this book may find themselves smiling at your entries, saying quietly "I never knew that!" And that in itself should bring you joy. I will ask you about your life lessons, and you may have to ponder deeply to respond. Or, you may be like many people who know them readily and can profess them with ease. Either way, we will take these pages one at a time.

When you are finished, your loved ones will know what your final wishes are, whom to contact, who is making medical decisions for you in the event you are incapacitated, where your banking accounts and safety deposit boxes are, who gets what, your favorite memories, your best lesson to pass on, and even the photograph you want in the paper for your obituary, and so much more. There will be no guesswork when you are done. And if things change along the way, this workbook allows for easy editing and updating of information. As each day is a new adventure and opportunity of living, this book too can take on a new life over time, reflecting the most current state of living and facts about you.

In the meantime, enjoy the sunrises and sunsets that each day offers. But while you are, be thinking about the wonderful gift you are creating for those you love and care about and the heartfelt tribute this book will ultimately serve to be when you have completed it and "made it yours."

SUNRISES OR SUNSETS?
By Holley Kelley

Which is more beautiful?
A sunrise or a sunset?
It depends on how you view them.
A sunrise boasts the news of a new day.
A sunset closes the day
but offers no promise of another tomorrow.
Is it more important to have seen
the promise of the day?
Or to have lived the day completely
to the sunset,
just in case tomorrow never comes?
While they are both of equal beauty,
I like the sunset.
It tells me I lived my day.
I had the gift of that day.
I shall rest easy hoping for tomorrow's sunrise.
But, tonight I am grateful
for the beautiful sunset.

Getting the Most Out of This Planning Guide

This planning guide is an important project on which you are embarking. I urge you to set a timeline for completion to ensure that you do enjoy the benefits it has to offer. Perhaps you have just purchased this book and are browsing the various sections and sub-sections to get an idea of its contents and what it is asking of you. In doing so, set a flexible completion date. Maybe it's two months. Maybe it's four months. But have an idea of when you want to have responded to the sections herein with the understanding that you will want to continually modify and update this over your life's course as new information replaces old and your feelings and perspectives grow in new directions of self-discovery.

As a helpful gauge, when I work with clients covering the advance-care planning materials in this book, we typically meet once per week for approximately two hours to discuss the materials and consider the topics herein. At the end of our session, we select a task that can be completed independently before our next meeting. Typically, in eight weeks, following that format, we are completely finished with the various sections and celebrating their completion.

So, now seems a great time to ask you to get used to using YOUR book. How about completing your first entry? That's right! Get a pen or your favorite writing utensil and script in your projected date of completion here now— you can do it!

My projected date of completing this book is:

Oct 31, 2016

Wow! How hard was that? And, you have now officially begun this journey! Congratulations!

Remember, this book is of no use to anyone as it stands. YOU and only YOU bring this book to life and give meaning and character to it. It is like a "clothing free" mannequin without your contributions. Make each entry count.

When you put pen to paper here, ensure your moments are well spent. Let the true YOU shine through each entry as you ponder and complete the pages, particularly those of personal reflection and inspiration. Take the time to find that "right" photo you are referring to as you share personal memories or preferences. Take the time to say the words you wish you could in person. Do it in this safe place. Take action in a way that is meaningful and worthy of the task at hand.

I urge you to stop and visualize other people reading your entries when you are no longer physically here. Yes, that is painful—but, do it anyway. You will find yourself discovering a deeper sense of reflection that will allow your writing to reach a richer depth than you thought possible. While there are places for simple, even one-word answers in this guide, there are other places to pour out feeling with total abandon. You have nothing to lose and everything to gain. You can do this—one day at a time—so be inspired!

We should be taught not to wait
for inspiration to start a thing.
Action always generates inspiration.
Inspiration seldom generates action.
~FRANK TIBOLT

CHAPTER 1

Life Equals Death

To live is to die. Life's journey begins so beautifully with birth but simultaneously marks us with the fate of eventually dying. We don't know when that will be. We have no timer or stopwatch counting down the decades, years, weeks, days, hours, minutes, and ultimately the second of our departure. We just know there is an end "sometime."

For that reason, the best time to plan for your life's destiny is TODAY. This book is for EVERYONE who has reached the state of adulthood and is embarking on the wonderful journey of living. This book is especially important for those beginning their families and having children of their own. This book is all about planning for your final affairs, but it is absolutely about living too. So, young and old, this book is for you.

An unfortunate reality of society is that some of us do not live to a ripe old age. Some people are met with a fate of an early, sudden, and unexpected death. These circumstances are devastating in their own right, but they are even more so because the planning facets of those younger lives are often not in place.

I urge users of this book to begin this book NOW. If you are in your twenties, thirties, or forties, there is no better time for such planning initiative. Of course, we know we should put our final wishes in order in later years. But if we do so early, we have all bases of life's unexpected circumstances covered.

Some of these obligations are difficult topics and undesirable considerations. But, I suspect once they are faced, they will no longer have the negative influence over you that they once did. The power is in the planning. To consider a young mother, wife, or daughter tragically killed in an automobile accident on her way to work one day is a devastating thought. The many crosses and memorials we pass while driving down the highways serve as a constant reminder to us that tragedy can strike and loss can occur randomly and unexpectedly. Realistically we must recognize that in life there are certain events over which we maintain little control. However, you can take control of nearly every subsequent occurrence that could surround such a terrible event.

Consider the same young mother and imagine that instead of being killed in a car wreck, she is alive but fighting for her life. What would she want? What would you do if this were your mother, wife, or daughter? Most of us cannot say what we would do, not only because we desire not to consider such dreaded situations, but also because we really do not know. But YOU know what you would want to happen if this were you. And if you don't, you will figure it out as we consider and explore various situations more in depth in this planning guide.

Yesterday is ashes.

Tomorrow is green wood.

Only today does the fire burn brightly.

~ESKIMO SAYING

While planning for our final wishes seems to be associated with a need of the aged and elderly, nothing could be further from the truth. The time to plan is now.

To live is to know we are predestined to die. I continue to repeat what we already know for the reason of simply reminding YOU that avoidance will not make it go away. So, why not be prepared?

If you knew you had twenty people coming over for dinner tonight, what would you do? You would plan your evening, pencil out a menu, make a list, go to the grocery store, and buy the food to prepare your meal. You would also think about what you would wear and coordinate your timing to ensure you have ample preparation and cooking time. You would ensure every detail was in place so the meal was hot and ready to serve when it is time eat. You may even think about engaging conversation or other fun things you could incorporate into the evening so everyone involved has a good time. You would tidy up your home, arrange appetizers, and meticulously set the table after choosing just the right linens and napkins. Wow, there is a lot that is going into your dinner party!

This planning guide is very similar to the coordinating of the dinner party. There are several layers of planning and details, and each one should be met with the overall goal of a successful outcome that is pleasing to you and others who participate in your life.

In the end, NONE of us get out alive. That is not a gloomy outlook—it is simply the reality of it. It should only remind us that every single day is an absolute gift of life! How lucky we are to have the immense opportunity of thriving, growing, and learning in the everyday joy of life!

Why You Should Plan

The reasons to plan are two-fold. First, it allows you to be the decision maker about what happens while you are living and after your death. You will be able to consider various situations and determine your thoughts and feelings and put them into writing. Most of what you put here in this life-planning book will be used. Remember, we have already established we will all die one day. My hopes, of course, are that we will all live a wonderfully long and satisfying life and make it to 140 years old and pass in an instant with a smile on our face. But that is only my wish, and a higher entity will dictate the details and timing surrounding our individual exits.

The second reason to plan is to lovingly and thoughtfully remove the burden of guesswork and confusion from those who love you so deeply. When this book is actually used to determine your thoughts and wishes, your loved ones will be in great agony and despair. Their emotions will be tested and their hearts will be broken. To burden them with additional decisions is the last thing you would want to do. That is why putting your wishes down clearly in writing frees them from the unpleasant duty of predicting what you would have wanted. There will be no guess work. There will be no turmoil regarding decisions. There will be no animosity among relatives speculating about your wishes. You have given them a user-guide for your "what-if" scenarios of all kinds. You have given them the gift of planning.

You already know why one should plan his or her final affairs, and you already know YOUR reasons or you would not be reading this book. We all know of someone or a situation in which a tragic event was only worsened by lack of prior planning by the deceased. We have heard of families feuding and at war in total disagreement with regard to a loved one. We shake our heads in a quandary wondering how the focus can get so far from the person that really matters and who more than ever needs everyone's united and loving support. The reasons to plan are simply endless. But your reasons for planning are unique to you.

It seems appropriate here to share a story about the parent of a close friend of mine. His mother was a vibrant, healthy, and attractive woman: a mother, wife, sister, and grandmother who at the age of 83, was working every single day in the family business.

Unfortunately, one routine trip to the doctor revealed that she had stage-2 colon cancer. She, with her husband of 51 years, had consultations with her doctor and met with the surgeon. It was determined that a colon re-sectioning was to be done; and she would be back to living a normal life, once she recovered from surgery.

I recall her personal outlook on this was "let's get this done so I can get back to living." While I am positive she was worried, she worked right up to the end, remaining calm publicly, hoping to shelter others from undue concern.

The surgery took place and though challenges were encountered, it seemed to have been successful. Her husband, by her side, gave the family the much anticipated news of her success. Unfortunately, the following day, another phone call came to family members stating that she had been taken back to emergency surgery due to a perforated section of the bowel, which was causing leakage and needed to be fixed immediately.

Prayers were offered, and family members remained hopeful as they waited. The following day her fever spiked indicating infection and she was given antibiotics. Since she had undergone the initial surgery, she had not yet communicated well with family members. The back-to-back effects of anesthesia are often cognitively debilitating, and the impact of such is typically exacerbated with age. But, that was something they could live with. They just wanted their mother, sister, grandmother, wife back. They needed HER to be okay.

Two days after the second surgery, her husband agreed to return her to the operating table because the infection had worsened, to allow the surgeon to go in yet a third time. Every surgery seemed to do more damage than good. This 83- year-old beautiful lady—who had entered the hospital strong, fit, and exuberant just days earlier—was now a fragile, drained and delicate being fighting for her very life.

But, she was no weakling at heart, and her family knew despite what had happened thus far, a bold and fearless warrior existed in that little body; and they prayed she would prevail in the end as she narrowly clung to her dwindling existence.

Her family was her priority in life. Her three boys, all grown and enjoying adult lives of their own, brought her great pride and joy. Her siblings, three brothers and four sisters, remained extremely close in their older years, always planning social events, family reunions, cruises, and vacations. They were living the American dream of the golden years and sharing every experience together that they possibly could. This was a "golden girls and golden guys" club of siblings if it were to be labeled.

To be conscious that we are

perceiving or thinking

is to be conscious

of our own existence.

~ARISTOTLE

Her husband often did not go on these trips with her. Those most intimate in her life knew the reason, though it was rarely spoken. The early years of this marriage were not as harmonious as they should have been. It seems the man she chose to stay with for over 50 years had a history of violence and abuse. One of her brothers recalled having to drive across several states to come to her aid and support following some of these abusive episodes. She never reported him. Her family never forgot.

Instead of harmoniously melding over time as often occurs, they became emotionally estranged. They lived together under the same roof, enjoyed friends together, shared a social life together, and kept up the facade in hopes the world would believe all was well.

As she had gone through life wearing countless pairs of rose-colored glasses, she viewed the surgery with the same positive yet unsuspecting outlook. In doing so, she discounted any pre-planning of her personal affairs. Perhaps doing otherwise would have silently acknowledged the possibility of a forbidding outcome. So instead, she did what she had always done: remained confident, optimistic, and passively status quo.

Immediately prior to her being admitted to the hospital for surgery the various forms were completed by her husband who relieved her of the burden. In doing so, this action also established him as the primary decision maker and single authority for all medical decisions. By not handling these matters well in advance, the entire sum of her life was in the hands of her husband. But, this was a needless concern to her as she was going to be fine, and he did love her. Their marriage, which was once hostile, had come to a place through the years where earlier concessions had long been swept under life's large Persian rug of oblivion. So, having him in charge of all of her medical decisions seemed appropriate. But was it?

Her family would say otherwise. The third surgery was a final effort to fix what had been the result of previous medical blunders. Deterioration and infection of the tissue was so severe that the once stable flesh was now giving way like a saturated Kleenex. Her chance of survival at this point was less than one percent.

Life is a train of moods like a string of beads,
and, as we pass through them,
they prove to be many-colored lenses
which paint the world their own hue,
and each shows only what lies in its focus.
~RALPH WALDO EMERSON

Her family continued to pray. At times, she was coherent which encouraged their hopes for her recovery. She was the kind of person about whom you hear people say, "If anyone can make it through this, it's her!" The glimmer of optimism was the possibility that her body could actually do the healing itself. And, we all know that our bodies, powerhouses of possibility, often go beyond medical science and perform miraculous feats often unexplainable by medicine, reason, or our mortal understanding.

She wanted to live. She was lucid at times and had heartfelt conversations with those beside her. She would share events of her "time away." That is, her memory of her subconscious events and some were even quite humorous.

I personally asked her if she had experienced "crossing over" or seeing any "white lights?" She indeed shared that such events had occurred. She stated that she left her physical body and could see herself below. On the "other side" there was a welcoming party for her. She admitted to knowing none of them. But they were nice and she felt as if she were among friends. She also shared they said, "We've been waiting on you. We're glad you're here!" They then asked her to come with them and she saw a bright light beckoning, which they asked her to follow them towards. Then she stated that she said, "No way! I'm not ready for this! I'm not dying! I'm getting the hell outta' here!" And, we all laughed with her at her rebellious spirit which reigned strong even in the face of benevolent Divinity. We also loved that story because it showed us she was in the fight to win it. She had not surrendered to the notion of dying. She also said she just wanted to get better so she could "go shopping at Macy's," her ultimate favorite pastime.

Hope is a strange invention-

A Patent of the Heart-

In unremitting action

Yet never wearing out....

~EMILY DICKINSON, c.1877

She was getting better. She would live. She would go shopping at Macy's again. Spirits were tested and hope prevailed. But, things quickly changed. She was not improving despite being able to move from a bed to a chair and eat a little Jello and drink some water—gigantic milestones after coming face-to-face with her mortality just weeks earlier. The reality was her colon was permeable, trickling waste throughout her body, poisoning her slowly to death. While her spirit was prevailing, her body was only able to endure so long. Sadly, the infection gained momentum and took her wonderful and lively spirit hostage. She was weak and only had short spurts of strength where she would visit with her loved ones.

Decisions had to be made and her sons and siblings wanted to be involved in that process. But, her spirit was not the only thing taken hostage. Their voices had also been imprisoned. Since the onset, her husband had become secretive, ordering doctors and nurses to tell nothing to his wife or any other relatives, including her sons. Closed-door meetings chafed family members who wanted to be part of the vital decisions regarding her life. Conflict was on the rise and discord abounded as a family of over a dozen members stood opposed to the authority of one single man. They strategized as to how to overrule him, reason with him, or appeal to him. They stood by as he made decisions that they didn't agree with but even worse, that they KNEW she wouldn't have wanted.

Everything in human character
goes to wreck, under the reign of procrastination,
while prompt action gives to all things
a corresponding and proportional life and energy.
~WILLIAM A. ALCOTT

Her family was horrified as they said to one another, "She wouldn't have wanted it this way!" But, what they weren't saying was, "I wish she had planned. Why didn't she plan? She should have planned!" Unfortunately, this story does end tragically, as you probably expected. She continued to decline.

I remember standing next to her bed, coaching her to hang in there, not to give up. I reminded her that we had to go shopping at Macy's and hit the big sale. She looked up at me, listless and weary and said the worst thing I could hear in that moment, "I don't want to go to Macy's. I don't want to go shopping anymore. I don't want to live like this. I'm tired." I discounted her words as if they had no merit and had never even been spoken and said, "It will be fine. We will help. It can be done!" She replied lifelessly, "I'm tired of fighting. I'm ready to go." I had heard her. Her family had heard her. But she had declared what nobody wanted to hear. Surrender. The brave warrior of previous days had finally waved the white flag of defeat.

The time had come to make the difficult decision of withholding food and nutrition in an effort to ultimately end her state of living. In essence, or laymen's terms, it is starving one to death and not unheard of medically as it relates to the final days and hours of one's mortal life. It is a controversial topic to those for and those against this approach in dealing with terminal illnesses and ending suffering. But, such controversy is heightened when it is your family member, your mother, your sister, your loved one.

As you can imagine, the family walls came tumbling down like the walls of Jericho when her husband made the decision to withhold fluids and nutrition. Those in opposition were overcome with sadness and anger. The family had only one reality that remained and that was to cohesively share in waiting for death to arrive. And, death did befriend this beautiful lady in early October, less than three months after what was supposed to have been a quick, straightforward surgery.

I wish I could say that the story of this turbulent event surrounding this remarkable lady ended there. But, rifts continued about the burial plans and arrangements. The husband wanted things handled quickly, economically, with no ceremony or memorial. She would be cremated and he would keep the ashes. The family was devastated at the thought of this. Just days earlier in the presence of her son, her husband stood at her bedside as she bravely accepted her own death. She sadly and thoughtfully professed her last and final requests knowing they would bring her peace and her family closure. He looked into her beautiful trusting brown eyes and fraudulently promised to honor each of her final requests. He stood by her death bed and lied to her.

You may delay,

but time will not.

~BENJAMIN FRANKLIN

But, her boys weren't ready to surrender yet. While their ultimate battle had been lost, and they were now laying their beloved mother to rest, they planned to take a stand for her last wishes. In the end, they did get the father to come around to some of the wishes she wanted. Other parts were never carried out, including releasing some of her ashes for her brother to take to North Carolina to spread over her parents' graves. The tired and frustrated boys did the best they could in the circumstances, and I have no doubt their mom would have been proud.

This story is shared to illustrate how quickly things can escalate down a path of division, how a family unified can quickly turn into a family at odds. This story is shared to exemplify how important it is to plan ahead. But there are more lessons here that go beyond the basic principles of planning.

This situation could have possibly had a different outcome. Nobody will ever know for sure. Maybe your time is your time. I cannot say, nor do I know. But, I know the family of dozens of people in this scenario believe that if a different person had been given power of attorney, she might still be alive today as they feel the decisions may have made an impact in her survival. Hindsight, while it is often a clever teacher, equally offers painful clarity.

My destination is no longer a place,

rather a new way of seeing.

~MARCEL PROUST

Stress does strange things to some people; and clearly, this husband did not understand what the rest of the family thought was appropriate to handle this situation. Add a personality that is at odds, complicated, or a bit challenging and sparks can fly. The question is, "WAS he the best person to carry out those supreme responsibilities in this particular situation?"

I'll leave it to you to ponder your answer to that question. And, I understand that for most people, the answer is, "Yes, a husband is certainly the right person to fulfill that role." And, often times that is absolutely correct. But, what is important here is that thought is given to the question. It is a pretty important matter to deliberate for our own personal circumstances if there are doubts.

Everyone has strengths and weaknesses. Some people cope with stress better than others. Some people perform really well in a crisis and others go into a total meltdown. Some people are indecisive, others are decisive, some people research, and some listen to the experts and go forth accordingly. So, when choosing the "right" person to handle one's personal affairs, remember to choose the person that is right for YOU. It may be your husband. It may be your sibling. It may be your son or your daughter. It may be your mother. It may be your soul mate or your life partner. It may be your good friend. But, the best way to find out who it should be is to talk to that person about perspectives and viewpoints on end-of-life matters and share yours as well. You are probably best served by choosing someone you can wholeheartedly trust, whose views are similar to yours, or who is open-minded enough to honor yours even if they personally believe differently.

This is a surprisingly common matter. A friend of mine recently faced a similar situation with her mother who had been dating a gentleman for quite some time. When her health became an issue, she and her brother were concerned that she would allow her live-in boyfriend to make her medical decisions for her. They arranged a time when the boyfriend was not home to address their concerns with their mother, hoping she would not take offense. She didn't and she further clarified that her intentions were not to give him those rights and reassured her children that they would be in charge. This is just another example of how difficult conversations can open up dialogue and not only ease everyone's worries, but bring families closer.

Let our advance worrying become
advance thinking and planning.
~WINSTON CHURCHILL

I think the most important question you could pose to determine who that person is, is to ask yourself, "Who would be most anguished by my departure?" "To whom does my life mean the most?" "Who can handle the burden of such supreme responsibility?" There, I've given you the template for a very short list to work from.

The stories I have shared with you are unique in their individual circumstances and people involved, but not at all unusual in theory or universally for those who fail to plan for end of life matters. I have had countless people tell me how wonderful it was that, despite losing a cherished loved one, "at least their final affairs were in order. They made it so easy on us. We are so grateful they planned it all ahead of time!"

Anything short of that can mean the alternative, which can often end terribly. To provide a final ending on the first story, no, they did not live happily ever after. They continue to be a family divided. This further substantiates why I am so proud of you for embarking on the journey of this book. Together, we will pave a highway for your family to travel through the upcoming possibilities in the map of your life's future.

Pre-Planning Perpetuates a Peaceful Present and Passing

I personally feel that planning in our younger years is just as important as planning when we are older. Having said that, I recognize that those who plan in younger years are less likely to have their planning wishes executed. Most people do actually live to a ripe old age. But it is the high stakes of early, sudden, and unexpected death that remain vastly important here. Therefore, while the statistics show us that you may not have the greatest NEED to plan, you still have many REASONS to do so. If you are in your thirties, don't put this book aside until later. There is no day of the week with the name Someday. So, whether today is a Monday or a weekend day—begin this journey today.

Isn't it amazing how much
stuff we get done
the day before vacation?
~ZIG ZIGLER

I have stated many times that this book is for any stage of life. And, while you can celebrate initially completing it, it is a guide that you will be updating over your life. Life promises change. Perhaps your spiritual beliefs will change. Perhaps you will re-marry. Additional children could be born, or you could change your mind on types of burial preferences. All of that is fine and even expected. This book is here to grow and change as you do.

If you have just received a diagnosis from your physician and purchased this book because the content suddenly became relevant in light of newly discovered health information, planning might be timely. That does not mean you are making assumptions about your fate or prospect of recovery; it simply means you are being wise and proactive and ensuring all bases are covered in the best interest of you and those you love.

Completing this book is not surrendering to the concept of death. We did that the day we were born. Completing this book is a practice of intelligent personal business. This book will inspire you to live even more fully once you have considered your own departure. I predict that you will be inspired to find new joy and create new experiences that contribute to your well-being after you begin working your way through this book. That is the goal.

Ironically, this type of planning—that is planning for one's death, departure, end-of-life—we might as well hit it all head on—is often avoided due to its subject matter. But, you will experience peace of mind when the emotional weight that you were carrying without even realizing it has been lifted.

Death is no more than passing

from one room into another.

There's a difference for me, you know.

Because in that other room I shall be able to see.

~HELEN KELLER

CHAPTER 2

YOUR Thoughts on Living

Exactly where are you now regarding your thoughts on beginning to work your way through this workbook and guide?

You may not know the answer to that, but you do know whether or not you want to do this. Of course, whether or not you want to do it does not sway me from telling you I hope you will anyway.

By now I hope are you are primed and maybe even a little bit eager to begin the work. We will take it slow as we wade into these topics and you explore your own feelings along the way.

First off, you will be asked to write down what you are feeling right now about planning for your own end-of-life issues and evaluating your thoughts on many other areas of consideration. If we can figure out where you are today, we can navigate a strategy to design your plans for tomorrow.

Let's get started!

Attitude is a little thing
that makes a big difference.
~WINSTON CHURCHILL

WORKBOOK PAGES

Today's Date: _____

If you could choose three words to define your views on your life today, what would they be?

1. _____

2. _____

3. _____

If you could choose three words to define your views on death and dying today, what would they be?

1. _____

2. _____

3. _____

As you look at the six answers you provided, how do they vary?

_____

_____

_____

Why do you think that is?

_____

_____

_____

Life is a journey. We are all on a path simply by living. Some of us feel we are in a very good place and using the gift of each day to fulfill our lives with goodness and joy. Others feel lost or in a rut, perhaps lacking excitement about today and the future. Our life experiences, emotional outlooks, and personal and business circumstances greatly affect our perspective. And it all comes full circle because our perspective sets the stage for our experience. It's important to know where we are in our views and interpretations to be sure we want to keep heading in that direction or even perhaps forge a new path of self-discovery.

What are your thoughts on your current life journey today?

_____

_____

_____

_____

If you could change anything about your life, what would it be?

_____

_____

_____

_____

Do you believe this change is possible?

☐ Yes   ☐ No

Explain why:

_____

_____

_____

_____

If you had access to an unlimited amount of money, could/would that fix any issues in your life?

☐ Yes   ☐ No

How so?

_____

_____

_____

_____

_____

_____

You may be curious as to why I brought up money in the above series of questions. There is a saying that I have incorporated into my life: "If money can fix it, it's not a problem."

My perspective is simply that if the problem is one fixable by money, then it very well may not be classified as a genuine problem. All the money in the world cannot ensure perfect health. While money can be used to purchase health insurance that can treat and offer preventive care for certain illnesses, it cannot guarantee us good health.

> To expect the unexpected
> shows a thoroughly modern intellect.
> ~OSCAR WILDE

Money can fix a flat tire. Money can fix a late mortgage. Money can fix a lot of things. It is the things that money CANNOT fix that are life's genuine burdens. A broken friendship or dysfunctional family dynamic is one example of a burden that money usually plays little part in solving. Money doesn't eliminate grief, cure a broken heart, or turn poor self-esteem into a positive self-outlook. An individual on hospice cannot look to money as a way to change their circumstances. Money does a lot of things, including making life much easier when we have enough of it. But when I ask you to consider if money CAN fix the problems you face, it is simply to ask you to consider the true nature of your problems.

Often, our attitudes towards life's inconvenient and challenging situations hold an incredible amount of power over us and compromise our life experience—but, only because we allow it. Our attitudes make a bigger difference in our life experience than having any amount of money ever could. Have you ever met someone who had so very little in the way of worldly possessions, yet, despite having hardly any monetary possessions, financial comforts or luxuries, exuded the most incredible happy and cheerful spirit that it was nearly infectious and contagious? And, your mood was elevated by just being in their company? It is these beautiful people who have come to realize that a rewarding and meaningful life isn't bought. That life already exists in each of us, ready, willing, and waiting to be treasured. A positive attitude is central to how we view our life. Often when life changes, so does our perspective. Sometimes that is for better. Other times, it is for worse. Being aware of how our individual perspective relates to a situation is highly important in how we regard that event or reality. But the beauty of this is that we're in charge! Change your perspective, change your life.

Money may be the husk of many things
but not the kernel.
It brings you food, but not appetite;
medicine, but not health;
acquaintance, but not friends;
servants, but not loyalty;
days of joy, but not peace or happiness.
~HENRIK IBSEN

What accomplishments in your life are you most proud of?

_____

_____

_____

_____

_____

_____

_____

_____

_____

_____

_____

I have given you plenty of space here because while you are probably just abbreviating and hitting the highlights, there is much pride in the life you have lived thus far.

What in life do you WISH you had done, but never did?

_____
_____
_____
_____
_____

Now that you have written that down, do you feel it was achievable? Do you have regret? Do you still want to pursue this dream? (Explain)

_____
_____
_____
_____
_____

Do you feel you are living your life to your fullest potential?

☐ Yes   ☐ No

If no, what changes can you make to live a fuller life today?

_____
_____
_____
_____
_____
_____
_____
_____
_____

What are your top three worries?

1. _____

2. _____

3. _____

What, if anything, could be done to alleviate these worries?

_____

_____

_____

_____

_____

_____

Are these worries affecting your quality of living today?

☐ Yes   ☐ No   ☐ Positively   ☐ Negatively

How so?

_____

_____

_____

_____

_____

Why do you want to plan for end-of-life issues?

_____

_____

_____

_____

_____

_____

_____

_____

We all have worries. While we can rationalize that worry is often a near use-less and unproductive emotion, it is so very difficult to escape. The Dalai Lama XIV said, "If a problem is fixable, if a situation is such that you can do something about it, then there is no need to worry. If it's not fixable, then there is no help in worrying. There is no benefit in worrying whatsoever." Nonetheless, worries wear us down. Sometimes our worries are genuine and make logical sense, but they still do not do our mental, physical, and spiritual selves any service.

Other times, worry has clearly manifested itself into a habit that is just a diffi-cult pattern to break. In any event, worry can interfere with our quality of life. Other worries are so genuine and concerning that there is no escaping them. In the case of having a loved one with a terminal illness, that genuine worry and concern would be challenging to deny and is legitimate to worry about by almost anyone's standards.

However, many people often allow life's smaller inconveniences and concerns to define their life experiences. This practice hampers your ability to live a ful-filling life now. My only goal here is to distinguish between genuine reasons for worry and ones we have adopted because they have simply become a habit. If we can focus on our most vital issues and approach the day's smaller concerns with a positive attitude, each day can be more enjoyable.

Worrying does not typically change the outcome or circumstances, but it does change your actual life experience—and not typically for the better. So, if you are an incessant worrier, I urge you to stop the worrying and start the living!

It is never too late to be
what you might have been.
~GEORGE ELIOT

You have reached deep within yourself to think about things that you may have never thought about before or even may have preferred not to have considered at all. Doing so may evoke feelings of happiness or melancholy. But getting your personal feelings and thoughts to the surface will help you understand yourself better concerning where you want to go from here. Every day is a new day!

CHAPTER 3

YOUR Bucket List

Most of us have plenty of things we aspire to do in our lifetime. Often, these special milestones or wishes are postponed to the future as life often gets in the way. These things are often referred to as a "Bucket List." A Bucket List is a list of the things you wish to do before you, well...to use the slang term, "kick-the-bucket."

Ironically, the term Bucket List comes from the idiom "kick-the-bucket" which has the intended meaning of "to die." "Kicking-the-Bucket" is said to have many possible unverified origins.

One theory is that in medieval times, people stood on a bucket prior to a hanging and the bucket was "kicked" to perpetuate death by hanging. Another theory is that the saying began as an early Catholic custom of holy water buckets that were placed at the feet of a deceased individual. The patrons would then sprinkle the holy water on the corpse as they paid tribute to the person who had passed. Regardless, a bucket is meant to be filled. Your Bucket List can be filled up with all of your future aspirations and wishes. You can fill the bucket, completing your items one at a time and thus have fulfilled your Bucket List. Or, your other choice is to kick the empty bucket around and never fulfill any of your dreams, almost like kicking a tire to imply you are doing nothing more than wasting time. If you do nothing, you have an empty bucket only good for, well...kicking.

Regardless of its origin, your Bucket List is simply a list of those things you wish to do before you die. A Bucket List is about LIVING, though, not about dying. DYING is the deadline. It's that simple. What do you want to do while you're still here living? Do you know? Let's make a list!

Do what you can, with what you have, where you are.

~THEODORE ROOSEVELT

You probably have your own ideas already, but here are a few considerations:

~ *Is there a place you have always yearned to visit?*

~ *Is there a book or series of books you have always wanted to read?*

~ *Is there an adventure you want to participate in?*

~ *Is there a road trip you've mapped out or people or places to see?*

~ *Is there a television series, show, or movies you want watch marathon style?*

~ *Is there a class, course, lessons, or hobby you want to take or learn?*

~ *Is there something special you haven't done but always wish you had?*

~ *Is there someone from your past you need or wish to connect with?*

~ *Is there a dream yet unfulfilled that you need to plan and do?*

~ *Is there a charity or volunteer you have wanted to serve?*

~ *What is missing that you've always wanted?*

~ *Do you want to return to a place from your past to visit or pay your respect?*

~ *Is there something missing that you feel could compliment your life's journey?*

It could be simple. It doesn't have to be expensive. It doesn't have to be adventurous. It just needs to be fulfilling. For me, I actually want to go on a cattle drive at some point in my life. Now, I recognize that after twelve hours in the saddle, for several days, in the hot blazing sun, every joint in my body will ache. Only to be followed by sleeping under the stars with no comforts of a shower, memory foam, or air conditioning. It could be the lousiest bucket list idea ever! But, if I don't do it I will never know! And, we only live once! I do know one thing for sure; it will be memorable! What are your dreams?

Confusion is the welcome mat
At the door of creativity.
~MICHAEL J. GELB

My Bucket List!

1 _____
2 _____
3 _____
4 _____
5 _____
6 _____
7 _____
8 _____
9 _____
10 _____
11 _____
12 _____
13 _____
14 _____
15 _____
16 _____
17 _____
18 _____
19 _____
20 _____

Dreams Go Here

MOMENTS

By Holley Kelley

The inevitable awaits us;
but, it's time we do not choose.
So, how we spend each day,
and put each one to use
makes our life a story—the story of our truth.
Who we are and where we've been.
The choices we've made and all of our sins.
Each and every moment
affects the whole experience.
The time for change rests with us each day.
From the moment that we each wake,
we should think about the day we wish to create.
All those days equal the sum of our existence.
We should conquer each one
with dedicated persistence.
Time is dwindling—I hope you will listen.
We make this life what it is going to be.
From the moment of birth
till we rest under shady oak trees.
Fill it with goodness, gratitude, and joy
for your moments will tell
your whole life's story.

There are more copies of the Bucket List on my website so please access them. After all, you may change your mind. In fact, you may live life so fully that you move through one list and begin to tackle another! I am all for that. As you create each list, date your entries. And when you complete each milestone or dream, mark them off and date them as well. This will give you a history of achieving your life aspirations.

Congratulations! You have created a paper blueprint for living today and into the future! You have challenged yourself to make observations about your past, define your present, and plan your future!

My hopes are that some enthusiasm about life has stirred within you as you revealed your true aspirations for future living. And if you don't like what you have done in the past, well, it is just that—the past. It is time to move on to the important business of LIVING! We don't know how much time we have here on earth, so seize every chance you have to engage in your own life.

If you have unfinished business with regard to the past, that's okay too. We'll address that together in the next section as we explore your thoughts on dying and death. Yes, I do recognize that I covered the fun and exciting content of living first only to shift to the dreaded subject of death. You may wonder why I did this. It seems to make better sense that I would have begun with the topics of doom and gloom and ended on a happier note of new-found discovery and purpose. Without really defining where we are in the business of "living," we cannot interpret our outlook on dying.

Here we go. Let's get to the other side of this thing called "death." It is not a terrible fate reserved just for you. It awaits every single living creature. It is our inevitable fate—our absolute destiny. So let's confront it here and now!

Dying is easy;
it's living that
scares me to death.
~ANNIE LENNOX

CHAPTER 4
YOUR Thoughts on Death

Death. What an unsettling, dark, and disturbing word, right? Not necessarily. Actually, death is viewed quite differently around the world. Some beliefs and attitudes about death are positive, and certain cultures embrace death as a great journey into the next phase of life in which members will receive wonderful reward. While thoughts on death vary widely throughout the world, one common element seems to be loss. With death comes the sense of great suffering and grief on the part of those both experiencing death and those left behind following such passing.

We don't truly know what happens after death because we don't know of people who go back and forth between the states of living and dying. Of course, we have speculation, and most of us have heard the accounts of those who have died only to be resuscitated and share the story of their near death experiences, or NDE's, as they are termed.

Many of us also have religious and spiritual beliefs that define our theories of the after-life. Views on what happens after death vary from culture to culture. In reality, death remains a mysterious experience. Unknowns are scary in any situation. Think of the times in your life when you faced uncertainty and remember how you felt—a job change, a relocation, a divorce, your departure to college—any situation that puts us in unfamiliar territory is a bit intimidating. Death is certainly all of these things to many people: scary, intimidating, unknown, mysterious. And to add to the daunting thought of death is the idea that we have little control over its arrival. It chooses us; we don't choose it.

If you knew that you would live to be 110 years old and would instantaneously die (with a smile on our face, I'd like to add), would you feel differently about death? You probably silently thought "yes." So now with a timeline of great length, putting death far off into the future and considering you live to a ripe old age and even die with that wonderful grin on your face, we may be able to speculate that death is a little less frightening. What we have done in this depiction is remove the "unknown" we discussed earlier. Remember that scary situation we explored that left us in a state of no control? In the above setting we took the mystery out of death and made it a total spoiler, and we were content with that because it promised us a long and satisfying life; death was quick and we were happy.

> I'm not afraid to die.
> I just don't want to be there when it happens.
> ~WOODY ALLEN

Can't we get the same thing without knowing the specifics that are left to fate and a higher court? Can't we change our attitudes and embrace the idea that we are in control of our own satisfying and happy life and that whether or not death is quick or slow, we are ready because we have LIVED?

That is what I am trying to implore you to embrace. I want you to BE READY to die while you are LIVING. In doing this, the fears and worries associated with death and dying are lessened. Living a fulfilling life and planning thoughtfully for the end of life makes great sense. And, the reason is we just don't know, do we? While that's the reality, that's okay because there's a lot we do know.

We know that if we live each day to its fullest we are making the most of the life we have. We know that if we use the planning tools available to us, we can have faith and confidence that if a worst case scenario becomes reality, we have a plan that we have personally designed to our specific wishes. We know that avoiding living and avoiding dying don't serve us in living our best life today or dying with dignity and grace in the future. There's a lot that we can do for our best life now as well as planning for our inevitable departure.

Let's explore some questions on the topic of death in the following pages.

Dear Death

By Holley Kelley

Dear Death,
Who are you?
Why are you so cruel?
Why do we call you other names?
Is that our attempt to fool?

Dear Death,
You are a gypsy;
We never know where you will be.
A nomad, a wanderer—
When will you come for me?

Dear Death,
Are you our friend?
Because we've never met.
To me you are a stranger—
That scares me half to death.

Dear Death,
You are elusive.
And you're the one in charge.
Will you come in the morning?
Or, will you wait till dark?

Dear Death,
Perhaps you are peaceful.
You may be kind and fair.
I have considered this;
But I won't know till I am there.

Dear Death,
You are a mystery.
And one I'd like to keep that way.
Dear Death, we haven't met.
But I know we will one day.

WORKBOOK PAGES

Using some adjectives, describe your feelings towards death in general.

_____

_____

_____

_____

_____

Now describe your feelings and thoughts towards YOUR OWN death.

_____

_____

_____

_____

_____

How did your thoughts regarding death in general vary compared to your views towards your own death?

_____

_____

_____

_____

_____

Why do you think this is?

_____

_____

_____

_____

_____

Are you scared to die?

☐ Yes   ☐ No

If so, what scares you the most?

_____

_____

_____

_____

_____

Is there anything that could be done to alleviate some of the fears you have regarding dying?

☐ Yes   ☐ No

Explain:

_____

_____

_____

_____

_____

Are you more scared about your own death or are you concerned for those you would leave behind? Explain.

_____

_____

_____

_____

_____

Do you feel you have your personal matters resolved in preparation for dying?

☐ Yes   ☐ No

If not, what matters need the most attention?

_____

_____

_____

_____

Do you believe that planning your end-of-life issues will offer you more peace of mind about dying?

☐ Yes   ☐ No

In what way?

_____

_____

_____

_____

Have you experienced personal loss in your life?

☐ Yes   ☐ No

Did this loss change your attitudes about living and dying?

☐ Yes   ☐ No

If yes, in what way?

_____

_____

_____

_____

If you have experienced loss in your life, it probably set the stage for how you deal with loss and grief. In fact, it may still be an area of great bereavement and from which you have never really been able to recover. Grief and loss are absolute experiences of loving and living.

TRUE BLUE
By Holley Kelley

Much of my laughter
was inspired by you.
I loved you completely
through and through.
I walk through life in your absence
not knowing what to do.
I don't know where to begin,
or how to start anew.
I feel guilty being happy,
so instead I remain blue.
I sit here in this life—
a life I once knew.
It seems what I am feeling
is a love that was lost and true.
It seems what I am missing,
is I am missing YOU.

CHAPTER 5

Grief is a Thief

You may realize that your thoughts with regard to all death-related matters involve a sense of sadness and loss. This makes perfect sense. You may have pain and anguish in your life. It is a given experience for any person who has loved another living being. To live and love is to eventually hurt and experience sorrow and loss. This is also known as grief.

Grief is defined as keen mental suffering or distress over affliction or loss, sharp sorrow, painful regret. Not only do we grieve the loss of others, we also grieve our own passing in the case of a known terminal illness or suffering. There are various types, levels, and stages of grief; but they all equal the same thing in the end: devastation, heartbreak, misery, woe, anguish, unhappiness, and sorrow.

You may know this firsthand through personal experience, and if so you can identify with the pain that has become part of you from that experience. Some grief never goes away. Some grief is a reminder of what once was, and some even opens us up to live life differently as we evolve through the various stages of it.

The late Elisabeth Kübler-Ross was a pioneer in studying the field of death and dying and truly served as a human gateway for helping society come to terms with a dialogue on the topic of death, formerly a legitimately taboo discussion. She wrote several books and conducted studies on death. It was in her 1969 book, *On Death and Dying*, in which the five stages of grief patients experience were outlined: denial, anger, bargaining, depression, and acceptance.

One thing certain with regard to grief is that there is no set expiration date on it. It runs its own individual course with each individual. Grief can steal happiness and joy and can penetrate directly through the heart and soul of those who love and lose. If this is grief, how does one get to the other side of it?

Everybody suffers and grieves differently. Some people submerse themselves in a state of denial and push the pain to another place to cope and survive. Others cannot mask it or hide from it and are overcome by its grip. And there are those who recognize that recovery is a process that may never heal but that they must continue to live and find meaning in the aspects of their life that remain.

Grief is not necessarily a loss of life but can include a loss of what has been "our normal." We can grieve a career following retirement. We can grieve the loss of a spouse through divorce. Empty nest syndrome is a form of grief in that our children are embarking on their own lives of independence and we find ourselves alone again. And of course there is the undisputed grief resulting from the death of another person or thing we love and care about.

It is during our darkest moments
that we must focus to see the light.
~ARISTOTLE ONASSIS

To get to the other side of grief means moving through it, somehow and some way. And, for some—perhaps "getting to the other side" seems too tall of an order. But, you can find some healing with the help of loving friends and family. Support groups offered through churches, funeral homes, hospitals, hospices, and community support organizations are often critical in assisting people in coming to terms with grief. Grief can have a time zone all its own. It can grip us from out of nowhere, uninvited and unexpected. And, right when we think we're getting somewhere in dealing with grief, it can come knocking at our door all over again.

I mention grief in this book because the topic we are covering is all about living and dying. Both of those states create a considerable amount of grief. It is important that we both support others when we know they are coping with grief as well as give ourselves the support networks that can aid in our sorrow and heartbreak.

If you are going through grief, it is important to not go it alone and to be willing to get the necessary professional help to ease your suffering and encourage you back to a thriving state of productive living again. A call to your local hospital, funeral home, church, or hospice will lead you to many available options in the event grief becomes the forefront of your life. You are not alone in your state of grief. One of the best ways to cope with grief, sadness and loss is to surround yourself with others who are going through the same trials. Also, journaling your feelings can prove healing for many. Often the process of getting one's emotions onto paper can serve as a means towards acceptance allowing one to embrace his or her own state of living again.

Overall, grief has a strong hold that typically can be best managed through the support of others. If you face these circumstances yourself, be brave enough to seek the support you need.

I Meant To...

By Holley Kelley

What was your favorite color?

I really never asked.

And now it is too late;

the time has come and passed.

I meant to get advice—I meant to do a lot.

I knew we'd make the time one day,

but I always forgot.

We should have just sat down,

slowed down, treasured.

My regret for not doing so cannot be measured.

I want to know it all,

but you're no longer here to ask.

The lesson of remorse

is a difficult one to grasp.

CHAPTER 6
YOUR "Kick-the-Bucket" List!

We've discussed the topic of death and dying. You have answered some questions about your own feelings about both death in general and your actual future death. We have acknowledged that grief is a part of life and can greatly affect our state of living. So I have to ask you this next question.

Are you ready to die? I hear a resounding "NO!" I agree that you are just not ready! You have a list to make before you do! You've made your bucket list already and set the stage for living life forward. But, I have another important list for you to make. It's your "kick" the-bucket list! That's right. What do you need to do so you CAN die with peace and dignity?

I told you that your bucket list was about ***living*** and that ***dying*** was the deadline. Your "kick-the-bucket" list is about ***dying*** and ***living*** is the deadline. There are important matters that I want you to identify that need to be done not just before you die, but SO you can die with peace.

All the art of living lies in a fine mingling

of letting go and holding on.

~HENRY ELLIS

This list may contain things like making peace with a family member with whom you have been in a long-held feud and have wanted to make amends for quite some time. Perhaps your last will and testament is not done or needs updating, or you have not completed other such matters that you have inadvertently put off for too long. Maybe you have completed your will but need to share the news with family and have anguished over this. It is time to take action, and your first step is identifying the things you need to address. These are the things that need to go on your "kick-the-bucket" list.

This book is going to help you do some of the things on your list. But regardless of what this book offers, you still need to create your list. Write down all matters pertaining to your own impending peaceful passing. Think hard.

~ *Is there a phone call you have needed to make to an estranged family member?*

~ *Are there loose ends somewhere in your life?*

~ *Is there a sin for which you wish to have forgiveness?*

~ *Is there a confession that needs to be made?*

~ *Is there an apology long overdue?*

~ *Is there someone you need to show or tell what he or she really means to you?*

~ *Is there self-forgiveness that needs to be given?*

~ *Is there an unfinished project looming over you?*

~ *Are you personally gripped with guilt that you need to resolve?*

~ *Is there a spiritual or religious issue you need to remedy?*

~ *Is there a personal issue you need to resolve?*

~ *Is there a skeleton in your closet you need to face?*

~ *Is there a grudge that has gone on too long and you would like to call a truce?*

~ *Is there someone you need to forgive so that you can finally live in peace?*

~ *Is there something that is not right or robbing peace within your heart?*

This is the time to put these issues to rest, here and now! It is time to be free of your burdens. It is time to embrace the fullness of living. Life is short and apologies are pretty easy if you think about it. It's not the apology that's tough; it's more often the anticipation and anxiety of the unexpected outcome. Regret is some pretty tough stuff so get rid of your emotional baggage here and now! It's heavy and it's bogging you down! Send it packing and lighten your load!

So go ahead and get started. KICK your bucket!

My "Kick-the-Bucket" List!

Apologies, Forgiveness, and Amends

1 _____
2 _____
3 _____
4 _____
5 _____
6 _____
7 _____
8 _____
9 _____
10 _____
11 _____
12 _____
13 _____
14 _____
15 _____
16 _____
17 _____
18 _____
19 _____
20 _____

The fear of death
is the most unjustified of all fears,
for there's no risk of accident
for someone who's dead.
~ALBERT EINSTEIN

I asked you earlier if you were ready to die. I am quite sure every reader sounded off a resounding "No!" at the thought of this. I am now wondering if you believe it is a possibility that if you have peace about dying that you will feel better about the unequivocal notion of death.

Planning for death can provide a newly inspired perspective on living. In doing so, the "new you" following this project may be unrestrained, assured, with a renewed zest for living and in complete harmony with the life you have in front of you. So keep up the good work!

SECTION 2
LEAVE IT TO YOU!

CHAPTER 7
Advance Directives

You have come to the section where you will implement the many different considerations and factors we have been discussing. You will compile important papers and thoughts as they relate to your future goals and wishes. Some of the material you will complete independently and then place those documents in the notebook you have created separately. Others, you will fill in the templates as you gather details. The important part to remember though is that instead of leaving it to others, we're leaving it to YOU! YOU are the decision maker. You are President and CEO of your personal affairs and you are taking care of business!

You will keep copies of your forms, such as advance directives, wills, and other business related items. Some people also share copies of such items as advance directives with their medical care providers either willingly or as requested and needed. I am not a big advocate of distributing a lot of personal information needlessly. Remember that these forms can get lost or misfiled, so please do not rely on this system as your only means of disseminating your wishes. Additionally, when you distribute copies, you are no longer in control of destroying older versions as you make updates. Therefore, the most updated hard copy needs to be accessible and available in the event of an emergency. Please designate whom you will tell this information to and secure a plan for them to access the forms.

It is time for you to make some tough decisions related to both living and dying and go through the actual emotions of putting your thoughts in writing. Think about yourself and your personal beliefs if you find you are challenged. Also, consider your loved ones facing these posed scenarios; doing so should help direct your decisions.

Some areas may be left blank because they simply do not apply to you, but they are here to cover as many possibilities for varying individuals as are needed. You are now ready to embark on the completion of your Advance Directives. So let's discuss these important documents.

Don't waste your life in doubts and fears:
spend yourself on the work before you,
well assured that the right performance
of this hour's duties
will be the best preparation
for the hours or ages that follow it.
~RALPH WALDO EMERSON

What Are Advance Directives?

In layman's terms, advance directives are just as they sound...directives given in advance. It sounds quite simple, but the overall details of them can get quite complicated. That is why in this particular section, my goal is to introduce you to advance directives and to provide you the necessary tools to obtain and complete them for yourself.

The best time to complete your advance directives is when you are healthy. While advance directives often pertain to end-of-life issues, that is not the most ideal time to begin working on them and often proves too late in some situations.

Advance directives allow you to choose the type of care and treatment you would wish to receive regarding any life-threatening illness or medical situation. They also allow you to designate a decision maker on your behalf, should you be incapacitated or unable to carry out these decisions independently.

"Advance directives" is a term that refers to a set of planning documents that typically include a living will and a durable power of attorney.

A living will is a legal document allowing you to put in writing your wishes for various medical situations, including those considered life-threatening. You will make it known what, if any, type of life-sustaining treatments you wish to have in the event of a serious illness or injury.

A living will is often accompanied by a Do Not Resuscitate Order (DNR). This order will advise doctors and hospitals as to your wishes if you experience a life-threatening state, such as if you stopped breathing or your heart stopped beating. If you wish to be resuscitated in such a situation, your DNR would offer that counsel to your medical team. Other topics to address in a living will are your wishes as they pertain to hydrations, withholding food, and organ and tissue donation.

A Durable Power of Attorney (DPA) is a form that allows you to designate someone you trust to make health-care decisions for you. This would be important for someone in a coma, incapacitated, or experiencing mental or cognitive issues. A DPA is an important tool to allow another individual to serve as your health-care proxy or agent in the event you cannot speak for yourself. Overall, this is a useful form and one to most certainly consider having in place.

The legalities of advance directives are constantly changing. It would be impracticable for me to include the actual forms for each individual reader in this compilation. But there are ample resources available that allow you ease of access to these important forms, many of which are free.

Advance directives do not have to be complicated. They can be a simply written declaration of your wishes. But once completed, have them notarized and/or witnessed, and given to close family members and your physician. The separate notebook you have created should have a sleeve where you will place your advance directives and maintain current copies of them. There are also U.S. Registries that house advance directives. There are many ways to store them to ensure accessibility during a time of need. The most important component of advance directives is getting them completed.

Advance directives are not universal, and different states recognize and require different language and information. Due to the varying requirements, it is important that you access advance directives that are unique to your resident state as well as a second home or place you may stay for any length of time in your travels.

If you become ill in one state and have advance directives set up for another state, there is no guarantee that they will be honored or meet the legal requirement for execution. While there is an ongoing push for all states to share and recognize one document, it is unlikely that this will occur. There are many issues preventing uniform usage of these forms.

One important note especially affecting early completion of one's advance directives is that they can be changed at any given time. Therefore, as your life dynamics evolve and situations change, you can update your advance directives accordingly.

Please understand that other documents such as last wills and testaments are covered separately in this book but are still considered to be part of your advance planning. However, for the sake of this section, we are focusing on advance directives to include living wills, orders to not resuscitate (DNR), and durable powers of attorney (DPA).

When completing your advance directives, I urge you to review the documents in their entirety so you can deeply consider your position relating to the questions posed and determine your best course of action. The questions are challenging, highly emotional, and thought-provoking—evidence of all the more reasons these decisions do need to be made by you and not postponed only to serve as a challenging dilemma for your loved ones.

*Planning is bringing the future into the present
so that you can do something about it now.*
~ALAN LAKEIN

The following Caring Connections website, www.caringinfo.org, is an excellent resource for many end-of-life issues, including advance directives. Caring Connections is a program that is compliments of the National Hospice and Palliative Care Organization. They offer a comprehensive array of helpful consumer information, particularly details dealing with end-of-life issues. This website allows you to select your state and then print out the appropriate advance directive forms.

Another excellent resource, action and advocacy organization is Aging with Dignity, the creator of the Five Wishes living will. Their website offers solutions for living wills and can be found at https://fivewishesonline.agingwithdignity.org/. They offer versions available in nearly thirty languages, including Braille.

It is also worth mentioning that there may be other forms appropriate for consideration depending on your specific circumstance. For example, a Physician Order for Life Sustaining Treatment (POLST) form may be needed for people facing a serious illness. Because there are other forms beyond the basics covered in this book, it is always recommended that you consult your health-care team as part of your advance-care planning network so that they may professionally advise you. For more information go to www.polst.org.

The following site, http://www.nlm.nih.gov/medlineplus/advancedirectives.html, is a service by the U.S. National Library of Medicine National Institutes of Health (NIH) that provides detailed information as well as questions to ask yourself if you find you are unsure about how to respond to the challenging matters advance directives cover.

Because websites and internet addresses often change, the information provided herein could easily become outdated following publication. Therefore, please remember that a quick internet search or phone call to your individual state's Department of Human Services should direct you to the free advance-directive template forms for your specific state. Additionally, there are several other websites offering these forms both for free and purchase for consumer convenience, as well as the option to have your attorney draw up these forms for you for a fee. I also invite you to visit my website for current resources available on obtaining advance directives and to explore related topics.

CHAPTER 8

Last Will and Testament

What is a Will?

Much like advance directives simply meaning directives in advance, a will is simply that—your will. What do you desire? In more technical terms, a will or testament is a legal declaration by which a person, the testator, names one or more persons to manage his or her estate and provides distribution of his property at death.

Wills can be very simple or highly complicated and are often drawn up by attorneys. However, today there are many choices available to obtain a will that meets your individual needs. Each and every life is different, and various phases of our life course pose new and distinct issues as they relate to our possible death and those we would leave behind. When developing a will, these unique circumstances must be addressed.

Aside from basic personal details such as your name and address, a will should also contain the date the document was drawn up and signed. This is important for many reasons, but mainly wills are often replaced with newer and updated versions reflecting one's most current wishes. Therefore, it is important that the date be clear to establish the legitimacy of the document.

You will want to choose an executor of your will. This person is obviously someone you trust and feel is appropriate to carry out your wishes set forth in the will. It is typically recommended that you also give the executor the right to manage your estate. Having an executor can avoid legal setbacks and allow your pending personal matters, such as paying off any pending debt you may have and ensuring your financial obligations have been satisfied, to be handled expeditiously. Putting this in writing is important as it allows the executor to accomplish this task with your legal backing.

You will want to consider your personal property and how you envision this being divided and to whom it will go. The receiver of such property you designate is called the beneficiary. In addition, it is important to consider an alternate beneficiary (or beneficiaries) in the event that your original beneficiary has passed away prior to you. You will specify your personal property in detail and state the beneficiary (beneficiaries) accordingly.

> The present moment dies every
> moment to become the past,
> is reborn every moment
> into the future.
> All experience is now.
> Now never ends.
> ~DEEPAK CHOPRA

In the event of having minor children, you need to consider many important factors. If you are a single parent, you will want to select someone you trust to raise your children in a loving and nurturing environment in your absence. If you have a spouse, while you may designate that individual to carry out this role, it is important to acknowledge the possibility that he or she may die with you in an accident and not be able to serve in this capacity. Therefore, considering all "worst case scenarios" as they relate to your will is a cautious approach. You will also want to factor in money from your estate and how that money can aid and support the care of your minor children. There may be a specific age at which you wish to allow your minor child(ren) to manage those funds on their own. If you have life insurance, or a pension or other monies that would be available from the sale of assets, these funds can be allocated in your will according to your wishes to care for your children in your absence.

I have to mention another issue as well as it is occurring more often than you may imagine. There are people who view and consider their pets as children. In these situations, the pet's welfare, including financial support, must be laid out specifically in the will just as is done for minor children. There are also single wills and joint wills. How you choose to proceed depends on your individual circumstances and preferences.

It is important that the date and place you sign your will is specified on your will because this validates that you have done so on your own accord and serves as evidence that your completion was not performed under any type of duress.

There are two important things to remember: 1) to have at least two witnesses who are not beneficiaries and 2) to update your will as your life situations change in ways that may affect how your wishes are conveyed. Your will also allows you to list special requests and address other items of importance as deemed applicable.

Only put off until tomorrow
what you are willing
to die having left undone.
~PABLO PICASSO

Online Resources for Wills

For those of you wanting a DIY (Do It Yourself) last will and testament, there are ample resources online offering templates for wills for free or for a fee. When writing this book, I had originally hoped to provide everyone with the exact form they needed. This would have been next to impossible—well, actually it would have been impossible. I couldn't have done this. Everyone's needs are ultra-specific to their life and unique circumstances, not even taking into account the varying state laws and requirements regarding legal documents.

So, it became apparent that I didn't have to give up the notion entirely. I just needed to make sure each of you had the right tools to get the job done for each of the different circumstances you face for your advance-care planning initiatives. Wills can be obtained from your attorney. This overview of wills does not substitute the potential need for professional legal counsel for some readers. And I am positive many of you will skip the internet search and DIY approach and seek legal counsel with no "ifs, ands or buts," but the rest of you may take the "search, click, print, sign" method.

So, for those, a simple internet search in your browser titled, "last will and testament" will provide you with a multitude of options from which I advise you to choose wisely. You will want to be sure you are in compliance with your state of residence when creating your will so be cognizant of that when conducting your search. Wherever you go to access this important document, make sure it is the right one for your particular situation. Resources are also available on my website. One such site I discovered while conducting research for this book is www.free-legal-document.com. What is important is finding the appropriate forms for your particular situation, but know that there are many options available to you once you begin looking. When perusing these sites, take time to read some of the tips and suggestions which will help prepare you for the many decisions you will need to make before you prepare your will.

Where Do I Keep My Will When it is Complete?

Your will should be kept in a safe place that is accessible. The notebook you made should already have a sleeve specifically for your last will and testament. However, some people keep them in a safety deposit box or where their other legal documents are stored. The main thing to consider is ensuring that your will is accessible in the event it is needed. Some people officially file them with their local courthouse, but doing so can make updates a bit more challenging. Overall, remember to keep the most current copy of your will in a secure and accessible location and destroy older versions that have been replaced.

As we have covered, there are many ways to complete your last will and testament. If this means seeing your attorney, make the appointment. If a simple template will suffice, print one out and complete it as soon as possible. Don't put off this important detail of your life planning, especially if you have minor children. You will absolutely want to have a voice in the event you are not here to make those important decisions personally. Your will allows you this platform.

Your will is so important, that I am asking you to respond to the appropriate statement below:

☐ I have completed my will and it is current as of _____.

☐ My will needs updated and I will do so by _____.

☐ I do not have a will and will complete one by _____.

Plans are nothing;
planning is everything.
~DWIGHT D. EISENHOWER

CHAPTER 9

Final Wishes

What Are Final Wishes?

Final Wishes are the culmination of all the things pertaining to your final departure. They may include how you wish to be treated, medical care and life-sustaining protocols you wish to receive. Final wishes are the details outlined in your last will and testament, which will be executed as you have specified. Final wishes include your funeral arrangements or burial plans. They include your obituary and financial matters.

Your final wishes are everything you have made known in this compilation that you are creating and leaving as a road map for those loved ones who will follow each and every detail of your specific plan. It is your last assignment to them, if you will—your final request. But I want to make one important fact very, very clear. Just because you have laid everything out perfectly in writing does not always mean that each and every component of your instructions will go as planned. You may be wondering if that is the case, why continue with this book? But the truth is that life promises change. And, so does death. The best of plans have pitfalls and unexpected curve balls.

The most fundamental and essential advice I can give you goes beyond the paperwork. Discuss different components of end-of-life issues with your doctor and medical-care providers. Share your wishes with them and ask questions freely to obtain answers in areas you may not yet understand. Your doctor should be aware of your intentions as they relate to end-of-life care. However, it doesn't end there. I am asking you to talk, speak, and convey your wishes to your loved ones.

Whether they want to hear it or not, this is the best advocating you can do beyond this written work. And don't wait too long. There is no "perfect" time to have this conversation. Who wants to discuss her own death, and who wants to hear about a loved one planning for it? None of us, I assure you.

But, you will find that by introducing the conversation, something unexpected will happen. That is, the death talk has been done, and you have once and for all removed that oversized elephant in the room. There is a genuine sense of liberation experienced by both parties when the discomfort of the conversation is confronted and the talk has taken place.

So, you owe it to yourself and your loved ones to share with them this book that you are working on as well. The critical components of your final wishes contained in this book should not be a shock to those you love. You can save your surprises for everyone in what you reveal in your personal expressions that you decide to share inside this book. And when your end-of-life planning desires are known ahead of time, everyone can be prepared for what is to be done when the time comes.

Your shared time together will have more meaning once you have faced the challenging conversation of dying with your loved ones. And, more importantly, it solidifies your wishes beyond the paperwork and everyone is clear on what you have conveyed both written and verbally. This is the best approach for your plans to unfold as you wish.

Also, one final note regarding final affairs. This book is intended to prompt and encourage you to handle many of life's necessary planning initiatives. However, for some people and their unique circumstances, it will be necessary to go beyond this book and seek qualified financial or professional legal counsel. Some people have extensive assets or estates that would benefit from the professional services of an estate planning attorney. Others may need to seek the expertise of an accountant, CPA, or financial planner.

In such cases this book is still meant to complement other aspects of your end-of-life planning and also covers the very personal side of your life as well. If you have a twofold approach to your advance-care planning to get your business and personal affairs properly in order, that is perfectly fine. In fact, I am proud that you recognize your needs and are acting so responsibly on them! Definitely utilize the intimate and distinctive qualities this book offers to their fullest potential to provide a balanced approach to your professional business and personal planning. So, having said that, let's continue planning!

CHAPTER 10
YOUR Obituary

What is an Obituary?

If you say the word "obituary" very slowly, I think it sounds like, "I bet you are weary." I find that ironic, in that weary would definitely be a way to describe the state of many people when they are put to the task of writing an obituary. However, that won't be the case for you, as you will be encouraged and inspired to write your own!

An obituary is, simply put, a public notice of the death of an individual. It often lists the individual's name, date of birth, and date and place of death. It also includes information pertaining to the individual's biographical summary and is typically included in local newspapers in the obituary section. Of course, since we live in a technological world, these also end up on the internet as well.

For more detailed obituaries, it is customary that a fee is charged by the additional word or line beyond the courtesy notice of death allotted by the newspaper or media. Pictures and photos are often an additional fee as well. In other words, the longer the obituary and more information it includes, the more expensive it is to publicize it.

Who Submits the Obituary?

Typically, an obituary is completed by the family or survivors of the deceased individual. Often times, if the family is unable or not prepared to create the obituary on behalf of a loved one, the funeral home will assist them in the process and submit it to the media.

What Should an Obituary Include?

An obituary can be more than just a notice of death. It can serve as a loving tribute and allow family members to share the news of the loss as well as enlighten readers of the wonderful life lived by the individual.

A simple obituary, as stated previously, includes the name, date of birth, place of birth, and date of death, and it often includes age and place of death.

A more detailed obituary notice might also include the various places in which the individual had resided, business or professional pursuits, religious or church affiliations, hobbies, interests, charitable or non-profit causes supported, survivors to include spouse, siblings, children, grandchildren, and/or other people close to the deceased individual. Often it also includes place of residence for each survivor.

Obituaries can additionally include those beloved individuals who have died previously, such as a spouse, child or parent or sibling(s), and can be written as, "She now joins her spouse, _____ who passed on _____, following _____ years of marriage; and they are now reunited once again."

Obituaries can be creative sentiments and tributes or memorials to the deceased, or they can simply serve as a notification of the individual's passing.

What Information is Relevant to an Obituary?

What are you most proud of having accomplished or having been a part of during your life? The answer to that question should be something to consider including in your obituary. If it was your ultimate success or life highlight, it may be something you wish to be remembered for. For some, it could be a Pulitzer Prize or an Olympic Medal. For others, it is being a mother and volunteering at the SPCA. Everyone is unique and values his or her time on earth differently. But you need to answer this question, and then you will know what is relevant for your obituary. Think of your obituary as your condensed *CliffNotes* version of your publicly written legacy.

Additionally, the place you will be laid to rest is included in your obituary, as well as the listing of the funeral time and location. If you prefer donations to a certain organization versus flowers, you can list this as well. Samples of obituaries, both short and long, are provided in this section for you to review and to assist you in the creation of your own personalized obituary.

What Photograph Would You Like for Your Obituary?

A photograph included in an obituary is optional. If you wish to do so, you may want to make the selection ahead of time for your family. If you are in your thirties and working your way through this book, you may be updating your photo over time to keep it current. If you are elderly, you may want to go through the photos and decide how you want your image shared. Often times, when the task of identifying a photo is left to family members, they do not always choose the one that you may have preferred. That is why I encourage the process of individual choosing.

I have seen so many obituaries that announce the death of an elderly individual, and the photograph submitted is one of when they were a teenager or very young. That is certainly acceptable if the individual chose that particular photo for his or her own personal reasons. Perhaps that particular photo marked one of the best times of his or her life, commemorated a special occasion, or maybe it was the best photograph he or she ever took....regardless of the reason, just make it your choice.

Old photographs are fine if you want to capture a special time or be remembered in your youth. I always enjoy military photos of elderly people who have passed depicting them in their younger days serving our country with valor and pride. More recent photos may be more current but are not necessary. Your photograph just needs to be one that you like and that represents your personal desires. Leaving this task to family members makes it challenging for them and doesn't give you the option to choose.

I do not fear death.

I had been dead for billions and billions

of years before I was born, and had not suffered

the slightest inconvenience from it.

~MARK TWAIN

Who are Your Survivors You Wish to Mention?

This too is optional, but if you are going all out, you will probably include a list of your survivors. To figure this out, begin answering the questions, "Whom do you love?" and "Who is in your family?" These are typically the first questions to answer when considering survivors and loved ones you may want to mention in your obituary. And as mentioned previously, their place of residence and offspring can be included as well. It is YOUR obituary and you are the author, so include the people who matter to you. The individuals that you list in your obituary can be more than family members; they can be a life-partner, a dedicated and loyal work colleague, or even a caregiver or life-long friend. Give this some thought as it relates to who has been there for you and who is related to you and who really matters.

What Accomplishments Do You Wish to Share?

Did you retire after many years of service with a company? Did you serve in the military? Did you own/operate a business? Have you written a book? Do you love to read books? Did you raise three children to whom you are devoted and of whom you are proud? Did you volunteer? Do you show dogs? Do you enjoy baking? What are your passions? Are you a loving parent, spouse, grandparent? Were you an avid collector? Military enthusiast? Car enthusiast? Did you have a unique interest or talent? Talented musician? All of the events and pleasures that made you "YOU" are what you need to consider when contemplating what to share in your obituary. What you share doesn't have to be anything grand or special. But, it can be. Your obituary just needs to define the essence of you.

How big do you want to go? And, how much money do you want your obituary to cost? If you are interested, I encourage you to call your local paper before you begin writing your own obituary to get an idea of costs. You may get some information that will assist your process. Ask them how they charge, understanding that costs will certainly fluctuate from now until the fateful day that would feature your obituary. However, by getting an idea of costs, you may be able to better determine what you wish to include.

As mentioned earlier, some publications offer obituary listings for free, and smaller papers often charge less than larger ones.

It is also important to remember that some people have two residences and would like their announcement of death to appear in both of those places, or even in the place where they resided for quite a long time or even a birth place. This will be an added expense to factor in as well, if multiple obituaries are desired. I have included some samples for you to peruse and utilize as a template or guide to get you going on your ideas. These could easily be modified or shortened depending on personal desires.

Sample 1 Obituary (shorter version)

MARY MARIE BROWN, 92

Mary Marie Brown, 92, of Hope, Alaska, passed away on Wednesday, September 16, 2015.

Born February 14, 1923 in St. Louis, Missouri, she was the daughter of the late William Lee Hendrick and Kimberly West Hendrick.

She is survived by her husband of 56 years, Timothy Mark Brown; two sons, Mark Lucas and wife, Jennifer of Paduka, KY, and Cyrus Blake and his wife, Margaret of New Orleans, LA; a sister, Kimberley Jones of Merritt Island, FL; two grandchildren, Merry and Richard and four great-grandchildren, Trey, Lauren, Chelsea, and Robi.

Memorial services will be conducted at 2:30 PM Saturday, September 18, 2014 at Live Oak Funeral Home with Rev. Jimmy Kendall officiating. A graveside service will be conducted at 2:30 PM Sunday at Wayside Cemetery in Anchorage, AK.

The family will receive friends Saturday from 12:30 PM until 3:15 PM at the funeral home. In lieu of flowers, memorials may be made to the American Cancer Society, PO Box 1841, Washington, DC 55235.

Procrastination

is opportunity's assassin.

~VICTOR KIAM

Sample 2 Obituary (longer version)

PENNY RAE CONNOLLY, 69

Penny Rae Connolly, 69, of Kansas City, died at noon on Thursday, August 22, 2015 at the South Memorial Hospice in Kansas City, Missouri. She was born February 1, 1946 in Boise, Idaho to Bob and Kay Cleveland. She married Billy Connolly on November 30, 1968 and he survives.

She is also survived by her mother, of Spodunk, Washington and two children, Henry Connolly and Elizabeth Rae Connolly both of Gainesville, Georgia; two grandchildren, Kyleigh and Colton; two siblings, Robert Grover Kelly of Boone, NC; and Lidia Marie Goodson of Ashville, NC; one brother, Delano (Del) Kelly of Port Lucaya, Grand Bahamas.

Her father and one sister, Victoria Rainey Kelly, preceded her in death.

Penny was a life-long resident of Kansas City where she resided following high school and attended the University of Missouri and received her dual degree in Art and Primary Education at the age of 22. She graduated Magna Cum Laude and was soon hired at the Kansas City Art Institute as the director of Children's Artistic Endeavors. She was recognized on numerous occasions for her dedication to young artists and the development of art programs in public schools throughout the Kansas City area.

She loved to bake and was known for her special recipes and sweet concoctions enjoyed by her close friends and family. She also enjoyed quilting and collecting Hummel figurines.

The visitation is from 11 AM until 1 PM on Saturday, August 24, 2014 at the Seigal Funeral Home and Memorial. The funeral service will commence at 1:30 PM on Saturday, August 24th, also at the Seigal Funeral Home and Memorial. Officiating will be life-long Pastor and friend, Samuel Long. The burial will take place on the grounds of Seigal Funeral Home and Memorial directly following the ceremony.

Memorials and tributes may be made to the Kansas City Children's Art League, at P.O. Box 3333, Kansas City, Missouri.

The previous examples should shed some light on how much or how little information you might wish to include in your personal obituary. I have given you some parameters and options to help navigate your own path. I have also shared what is necessary to include in your obituary and the extras that can be included optionally. The rest is up to you. Now let's get some of the pertinent information down before you actually write your own obituary. Use the template below and complete the fields.

Checkmark your desired personal inclusions for your obituary and fill in blank(s):

☐ Name as you want it to appear on your obituary:

_____

☐ Date of Birth:

_____

☐ Place of Birth:

_____

_____

☐ Born to (parent's names)

_____

_____

☐ Survived by: (Who remains living?)

_____

_____

_____

_____

_____

_____

☐ Date of death unknown so leave a line in your obituary.

☐ Place of death unknown so leave a line in your obituary.

☐ Name of spouse (living or not?)

_____

_____

☐ If spouse, how long married or together?

_____

_____

☐ Name of child(ren) / residence city and state, if desired.

_____

_____

_____

_____

_____

☐ Name of grandchild(ren), if any (typically first names only and no residence listed):

_____

_____

_____

_____

_____

☐ Special family / loved ones who pre-deceased you (relation):

_____

_____

_____

_____

_____

☐ Career/Job/Educational information/Military:

_____

_____

_____

_____

_____

☐ Special causes or contributions, including social, civic, charities, volunteering, religious affiliation, philanthropy, etc.

_____

_____

_____

_____

_____

☐ Hobbies / Interests / Passions:

_____

_____

_____

_____

_____

☐ **ANY** thing additional you wish to include:

_____

_____

_____

_____

_____

_____

_____

_____

Visualize people reading this as you create it. You have just put your details down in writing. It wasn't that difficult, was it? And, when it is all said and done, aren't you an amazingly interesting person? Yes! So, write about yourself the way you really are!

Also remember that you are absolutely saving your loved ones from a challenging and arduous task by completing this ahead of time. The only remaining detail they will be left to add to your obituary will be the specifics of your memorial or funeral. The last thing your grieving family would want to be doing while suffering from the loss of you is having to be creative, all the while struggling to uncover the many pertinent details of your life in their efforts to pay a deserving tribute. By completing this, you are releasing them from this obligation so they can instead spend their time celebrating the joy of you as they support each other during a time of great loss and mourning. Clearly this is a worthwhile endeavor for you to complete.

Use the details you already created and write something special and unique that pays tribute to someone who has lived one amazing life—and that someone is YOU! You have gathered all the information for your obituary. Review your check marked obituary items you chose to incorporate on the previous pages. Make sure you're not missing anything. Now, it is time to write YOUR obituary!

You only live once--
but if you work it right,
once is enough.
~JOE E. LEWIS

OBITUARY

For: _____

_____
_____
_____
_____
_____
_____
_____
_____
_____
_____
_____
_____
_____
_____
_____
_____
_____
_____
_____
_____
_____
_____
_____
_____
_____
_____
_____
_____

Now that you have written your obituary, it would also be a good idea for you to make a copy of it and place it in your separate binder which will hold your other important paperwork derived from this book. If you are including a photo in your obituary, you will need to include this with your paperwork as well. In doing so, this will make things accessible quickly during a time of need.

Additionally, your loved ones will greatly appreciate that you have so thoughtfully prepared this ahead of time, saving them from this challenging obligation during their difficult time of loss.

To succeed in life,
you need three things:
a wishbone,
a backbone
and a funny bone.
~REBA MCENTIRE

CHAPTER 11
Funeral "Homes" and Finances

Surprisingly, many people actually know what funeral home they want to carry out their funeral plans. Some have pre-paid for such services, and some just know that familiar place they want to handle this important affair. Regardless, for a lot of people, the cost of funeral arrangements makes the short list of some of the largest expenditures they will ever make.

While we're on the subject, have you ever wondered why they are called funeral "homes?" It sounds quaint and inviting with a warm and welcoming atmosphere—a place where fresh tea and croissants are offered on a platter with a smile, and chatter about much of nothing is enjoyed and relished. Yet, it's hardly a place most of us want to call home. However, it seems that historically many funeral homes were often older homes utilized as funeral businesses, and in some cases the funeral director actually resided in the home.

Furthermore, since the deceased body would often be viewed in the parlor of the home, the term "funeral parlor" made sense even though parlor also refers to a business premises or establishment.

While commercialized buildings have predominantly replaced the neighborhood funeral home business front, it is easy to understand that a home-like atmosphere certainly offers some serenity to patrons facing the worst of times.

I recently spoke with a funeral home owner/operator, and he told me that it was important to him to make his funeral home inviting and welcoming. He wanted to ensure his surroundings were not dismal and gloomy. His goal was to incorporate as much pleasantness into his funeral home as he could. He said he decorated with colors that were determined to be mood elevating and therapeutically soothing, and he felt it made a difference in the experience his patrons had when they first entered his establishment. We associate the term "home" with warm and comforting feelings, and perhaps that is just the right environment to handle life's worst circumstances. So, it makes sense that "funeral homes" are still called what they are despite modern times and commercialization.

In any respect, the other detail I want to cover is funeral-home protocol. Funeral homes must adhere to common practices and procedures. This is a highly regulated industry. The Federal Trade Commission (FTC) passed 16 CFR Part 453 which offers a significant amount of consumer rights and protections and holds funeral homes to a high standard of compliance.

In addition, in this federal regulation, funeral homes are mandated to provide price disclosures; and consumers must be given price lists for goods and services such as ceremonies, caskets, transportation of the deceased body, and so forth. This is very helpful in allowing people to determine costs and make decisions based on their budgets and desires. In addition, federal rules require funeral operators to provide price lists over the telephone, making shopping around and comparing prices much easier for consumers.

Funeral Funding Considerations

There are many ways to pay for funerals or to allocate funds ahead of time to do so. While your options are plentiful, we will cover some more popular approaches for consideration in the event this is something you may want to do.

Some people choose to prepay for funerals and burials ahead of time. This is and has been a subject of ongoing controversy, leaving a significant number of consumers, attorneys, and financial planners both for and against this decision. Some elder law attorneys support prepayment, considering it a creative way to invest as it relates to planning for Medicaid and other factors in place such as Social Security. There is some consumer protection in place for those paying for funerals in advance, but there are still risks.

Some of the FTC's Funeral Rule is not applicable to some of the pre-need contracts due to individual state laws. Therefore, there are variances from state to state. In some states, it is required by law for the funeral establishment to put a percentage of the pre-paid funds into a state-regulated trust or to even buy life insurance policies and assigning the death benefits to the funeral home or cemetery of origination.

Funeral homes often have companies they work with to set up these types of trusts, but it is important that you understand all the facts. Some states have little to no protection for prepaid funeral arrangements. A visit to the Federal Trade Commission website would provide more specific details regarding your state's regulations on this topic. My goal is to simply make you a savvy consumer on this subject and offer you some basic information to ensure you have some background knowledge and can ask the right questions.

Some initial questions to ask are the following:

What are you actually buying and paying for? (Tangible items such as a casket, urn or vault, or services such as transportation, etc.?)

What will happen with the money you submit for payment?

Is interest earned? If so, what will happen to the interest income on this money? Who gets it?

What if inflation costs exceed your initial purchase or prices for services increase? Are you locked in or will your family have to pay extra for the services being rendered?

What protections are offered to you in the event the funeral business entity goes out of business or bankrupt, etc.?

Is there a refund option or timeline to cancel the contract? If so, what are the details?

What happens if you relocate to another area and pass away somewhere else?

If there's money left after the funeral expenses, who gets this money?

Is the policy transferrable to another funeral establishment?

You see where we are going with this. Knowledge is power. Once you have the answers, you will have a better idea of what you wish to do in this area of your pre-need funeral planning. It is recommended that you notify your family if you pre-pay for funeral arrangements, but this book will resolve that detail for you. You would be surprised by how many people actually pre-pay for their funerals and never notify the family. That is the exact opposite of the overall intentions. In the workbook pages of this section, you can provide the necessary and important details related to this topic so there will be no misunderstandings in your particular case.

Burial, Life, and Final Expense Insurance Plans

Another way to pay for funeral services is with life insurance that is specifically designated to pay for your final expenses. These are typically for smaller face amounts than traditional life insurance policies, and funds are often paid expeditiously upon one's passing to fund the important and immediate expenditures of the burial and service. As an insurance broker, I always felt these policies were a realistic way to offset the burden from loved ones.

I remember one very special client, whom I had the pleasure of working with, purchased a final expense plan. In his particular situation, he was not in the best overall health and purchased a final expense plan with a substandard, high risk, health rating. What is attractive about these particular final expense plans is that often they are a graded benefit structure, to mean that the maximum or full death benefit is not available the first year. It is a stair-step approach, typically a low percentage of the benefit is paid if the policy holder dies in the first year of issue, a little more in year two, and typically by the fourth or fifth year anniversary the maximum face amount is reached. This can be an appealing option for some people with less than ideal health conditions who cannot be issued typical policies. This gives the higher health risk policy holders a chance at coverage where they may have otherwise been declined.

This gentleman had a graded benefit burial policy. He knew he didn't have decades of life left, and it was extremely important to him not to burden his beloved daughter with the financial obligations of his burial. We stayed in touch regularly as he was always such a bright and cheerful guy to chat with. I remember he called just before Christmas in 2009. He had one important question to ask me, and that was, "When is my burial plan reaching its maximum benefit?" I asked him if he knew something I didn't know and simply laughed and jokingly told me that he just wanted to know how long he needed to live. On a serious note, he admitted that his health had been declining, he had home health care coming in, and his daughter was checking in on him more often to ensure his well-being.

I pulled his file and looked at the policy. We had a jovial conversation and I told him that he "needed to live until February 2010." He was happy knowing this as he thought he had another year to go until the policy reached its full benefit. We laughed and he said he thought he could do that. Late in February, 2010, I received a call from his daughter stating her father had passed away. I almost felt he had hung on just to ensure he made it to the finish line of his full policy benefits, and he was just the kind of guy that would have that level of staying power in the name of love.

Not all final expense plans are graded. But, for those who may think they are uninsurable, they are good to know about. However, the higher risk to insurance companies, the higher premiums they charge.

Another approach is simply to purchase a basic life insurance plan and earmark the benefits for your burial and funeral expenses. Term life insurance is another consideration, especially because of the affordability, but the concern with term life insurance is outliving the term (which of course is GREAT news but doesn't yield the return you were investing in). Some term life plans are renewable but often at much higher premiums and with new underwriting, so some people may not qualify or be able to afford the premiums.

Most licensed insurance brokers can assist you with determining the best value to meet your needs and discuss the suitability of the various life plans available.

Totten Trusts

A Totten Trust is a simple approach to setting aside funeral funds. Since it is technically not actually a trust and more a bank account, most banks can handle setting up this account for you in a short period of time. The idea behind a Totten Trust is to set aside as little or as much money as you wish to for future funeral expenses. You manage it. You would be the trustee and you can designate any person you choose as the beneficiary. There are some benefits to these types of trust accounts so if this interests you, you may want to talk to your bank or credit union. Also, it is important to shop multiple financial institutions, as some will offer interest at varying rates. In summary, upon your death, these funds are made immediately available to the "pay on death" inheritor or beneficiary to carry out your funeral wishes.

Medicaid and Funeral Expenses

If you are on Medicaid and interested in setting up a trust to pay for future funeral expenses, laws, rules, and allowances vary by state and are subject to change. Because of the complexity of this, you are encouraged to contact your state's Medicaid department and/or seek the professional expertise of a Medicaid or eldercare attorney to ensure the money you set aside is properly protected.

Veterans and Funerals

Regarding military funerals, if you are a veteran, you are entitled to a free burial, plot, and grave marker. This eligibility also includes some civilians who served in a military-related or public health service role. Spouses and dependent children are also entitled to a plot and grave marker in national cemeteries. While there is no current fee for grave openings and closings, vaults or liners, or setting the marker in national cemeteries, there still could be fees incurred for other expenses such as transportation or additional services or items incorporated. State veteran cemeteries are also opening; and while details, eligibility, and offerings vary, you will want to perform the same research on that as you would on most consumer goods you purchase. Some offer certain items "free" yet perhaps charge more for other important goods or services such as spouse burial plots, so ask many detailed questions to get the facts. The Department of Veterans Affairs has an incredible amount of information on this topic if you wish to delve further via the internet or they can be contacted at 1-800-827-1000.

Social Security and Funerals

Social Security will need to be notified in the event of death, and this report is often handled by funeral directors upon receiving the Social Security number of the deceased. When someone dies, it is important to contact Social Security as soon as possible to establish eligibility for any benefits, including a death benefit or survivor's benefits. There are many details surrounding eligibility as well as formulas and eligibility for survivor's benefits. You don't want to overlook this important part of your planning. Later in the book you will log important information regarding your Social Security details, making this easy for your family members to access if and when the time arises. Laws change regularly; so to learn more on this, visit the Social Security website at www.socialsecurity.gov or contact them at 1-800-772-1213.

We have considered some general information on funeral homes and some more popular ways to fund funeral expenses. If you wish to gain more information on any of the topics we covered, an internet search will easily reveal greater detail on any of these subjects. As I continue to share, this book is meant to be an easy guide for your advance-care planning. Keeping with those goals also means some of our topics are covered with brief overviews in hopes that the tasks of completion of your matters outlined in this book are ultimately achieved.

It is now time to switch our focus to a more personal level. That is, instead of discussing funerals in general, it's time to discuss YOUR funeral. If you are worried about what that entails, it's okay. You are more than ready to continue. You can do this. And, you are going a GREAT job!

Everything has beauty,

but not everyone sees it.

~CONFUCIUS

CHAPTER 12

YOUR Funeral and Ceremony

Have you ever thought about it? Have you let your mind wander to that unsettling thought of considering your own funeral? Some of you will answer this with an absolute "NO!" But, there are those of you who actually may have let your mind wander a bit and given contemplation to the reality of what is to come—your funeral.

We all will be departing one day. It is a big day, no doubt. But we also know it just does not seem to be surrounded with the customary celebrations of other big days we have had in our lives—the big birthday parties we have planned so meticulously, the anniversary celebrations organized in the most deliberate fashion, the events we have all strategically focused on to ensure the most wonderful outcome. Why is the thought of our own funeral such a downer? Well, for one, we won't be there (as we know ourselves to be). And, we are probably the life of the party, and yet we will actually miss this final event that is all about us.

We also know that all of the wonderful things that we have come to love in our lives are no more for us. We will not be there for all of the things we enjoy. We won't be at the birthdays, anniversaries, weddings, and even funerals. Being laid to rest is a really tough reality to embrace. I get it! But we can change our minds about how we view this day. We have the power to acknowledge all of the unpleasantness of death and dying and come to terms with it. It is important that we do this because it is happening either way. So let's spin this a bit. Let's wrap our mind around a different concept as it pertains to departing the mortal world as we know it.

Imagine you had never been born. What do you see when considering this notion? Who is now missing from the world? If you were never born, there are no offspring compliments of you since you were never here. If you were never born, your brother or sister would not have you as his or her sibling. Your parents, no daughter or son. If you were never born, how would the lives around you be affected without the presence of YOU? Your pet that you love and pamper and rescued from the dog pound, where would he be? Your grandchildren (or future grandchildren) that you dote on and love, where would they be? Oh remember, THEY don't exist because YOU were never here. The volunteering you do, the smiles you create, the life you live, and all of the ways you leave your mark on the world have ultimately and eternally altered the planet. You have certainly left your mark on the globe and forever changed human existence. Your life has made such a difference in the people and lives around you in immeasurable ways.

Just for fun, make some quick notes on what the world looks like, or doesn't look like without you.

WORLD WITHOUT ME, WHAT IS MISSING?

_____

_____

_____

_____

_____

_____

_____

_____

_____

_____

_____

_____

_____

_____

_____

_____

_____

_____

_____

We could go on and on with this exercise as we continue to think about our mark on society from the beginning. Your life has certainly unveiled new greatness to this world. But all good things do come to an end, and when your life does, there is clearly so much to honor and celebrate. I asked you above to consider the world if you had never been born to SHOW you, to PROVE to you the evidence that your life has produced great achievement and abundance, and with that impressive accomplishment comes praiseworthy admiration and deserving tribute.

Your funeral is the final celebration of your triumphs. For someone who has had such a positive influence on the world, you certainly deserve a pretty amazing farewell! So, let's start planning for a commemoration that you deserve.

Funeral Services and Memorials

Let's define the word "funeral." A funeral is a ceremony for somebody who has died, a rite held to mark the burial or cremation of a body, especially a ceremony held immediately before a burial or cremation. A funeral is also considered an end to someone's existence.

I know. It's really deep and morbid to discuss. But stay with me on this topic because it is important and it won't all be as bad as the definition sounds. I promise.

When you leave a funeral, do you usually think the person laid to rest would have been pleased with his or her farewell tribute? I always say that there is little in life more sobering than a funeral. It puts us pretty close to that "inevitable" we like to ignore. We know that we too will one day be there. We don't like funerals because they remind us that our time here is limited. And of course I am not even addressing the terrible loss of those close to us whose funerals are sorrowfully and remorsefully attended.

While I have been to many funerals, very few have I gone to that I actually left truly feeling that the ceremony was a wonderful glorification of the person's life. More often than not, I feel as if the deceased individual had been slighted without genuine honor and praise. Personal tribute had been diluted with generalizations that could have pertained to anybody. In general, I have left most funerals recognizing the sadness of the loss, but feeling as if the person who had passed was cheated out of his or her death-day tribute.

I have found many funerals to be little more than an entire life culminated in thirty minutes of generic commentary in a canned farewell from a preacher who has done this more times than he can count.

In these instances, I feel disappointed for the individual, the families—though they are often in such a state of grief they probably do not recognize the shortfall—and, of course, the guests in attendance. Some patrons are close personal friends who knew the person well. Others are distant acquaintances who come to offer support and condolences. And yet, when they leave following the ceremony, they unfortunately know no more about the deceased than they did before.

News flash! Your funeral doesn't have to be that way! And, it won't! Because you are planning it! That's right; you are the playwright of this production. So get your creative groove on, and let those inspirational juices begin to flow. You are going to have a five-star performance when you are done. The reviews will be in the form of laughter, smiles, tears, and deep personal reflection. When you're done—literally—and when you're done with your guests in attendance, they will be moved. They will know you. They will be inspired by you. And part of you will leave with them!

Remember at the beginning of this section we said you wouldn't be there? Well, I've got news for you! You'll be there all right, and in each and every detail, you will make your presence known. Just as if the director of a play is present for all the rehearsals and just misses opening night, he still has his fingerprint on each and every performance. And, similarly, so will you!

A funeral has no business being boring. People aren't boring. You aren't boring. So, why should life's last retirement party not be full of festivity, activity, and even some surprises?

Okay, so I've hopefully inspired you to be creative. But having said that, you still have many, many decisions to make. We will complete some workbook pages to establish your thoughts, wishes, and preferences in some areas. And for others, we will help you by providing useful information related to your abundance of choices. You may already have a vision, and that will help. But if you don't, do not be concerned! We will figure this out together.

I do want to share one story here for those of you who feel your life may not be deserving of this death-day tribute we have been discussing. Maybe you don't think you've done enough interesting things. Maybe you don't think you're very creative. Perhaps you do not have a big circle of loved ones to attend. Maybe some relationships are strained. It is not at all uncommon to feel this way and question the notion of creating your own meaningful funeral.

Many years ago, in addition to my full-time career, I began performing funeral services. In this capacity, I would be considered an "officiator." In this role, I would meet with the family and gather pertinent details regarding the deceased and use that material and their ideas and suggestions to create a funeral service or eulogy that I would officiate or deliver.

My very first call following my solicitation of offering funeral services is one I will never forget. The funeral home contacted me and stated that the family wanted something "a little different" and that there was a lot of "unusual" family dynamics taking place with regard to the father who had passed.

This was my very first request to officiate at a funeral, so of course I was happy the phone was ringing! In retrospect, I now realize it had nothing to do with my proclaimed writing, speaking, or marketing ability; and the truth was that the funeral home just didn't want to deal with this. I was asked to contact the family, and it was evident that the funeral director felt this was going to be a difficult matter to accomplish. I should have known when he sarcastically said, "Good luck with THIS one!" that I was in for something challenging.

Upon calling the family, I learned a lot. But what I realized rather quickly was that the family did not really like the father very much. In fact, they seemed to find him rather detestable. I was not even sure if they were upset about his passing. There had been an incredible amount of estrangement, and this was not a man for whom they harbored the greatest affection. They almost appeared put out by having to have a funeral and even honor him but felt it was a ritual they could not overlook. I quickly began to wonder what I had gotten myself into. But, I had a job to do, and despite the challenges, I had to find something redeeming about this man who had just died.

I asked many questions that I would later use to write the ceremony. I learned that they described him as a miser. He was selfish and impatient. He was a retired military colonel, and while he was not affiliated with any particular religious faith, they stated he was "into" wizardry. I remember as they were telling me all of this, I was shaking my head questioning what on earth I was ever going to do with this! I did not have any idea about wizardry! And, I didn't know how to make a funeral wonderful for a man it seemed everyone hated! This was a celebration all right, but not a celebration of his life. It was a celebration that he was gone!

Surprisingly, the answers to my questions continued to reveal a pretty interesting guy. I was intrigued at this life that was clearly both frustrating and perplexing to his children and close family members. While I was unfamiliar with a lot of what was shared, I had two unwavering goals, and that was to give this gentleman the funeral he deserved and to allow his children to hear from him one last time.

I found many interesting and unusual facets of this gentleman who had been deemed "difficult" at a minimum by his survivors. I put together a very nice service on his behalf and delivered a eulogy that may have even made him smile. I found there was a significant amount of "good" I could uncover in all of the negativity.

I shared with the patrons things they may not have known about him. He had maintained a highly successful role in his military career and served his country with dedication and valor. I shared the realities that he may have been challenged with fostering and developing enriching personal relationships with those closest to him. I recognized that following such a high-ranking and consuming profession, retiring probably proved incredibly difficult and more than likely led to his reclusiveness. I discussed the interesting notion of wizardry that actually ended up being less bizarre than I first thought. I read pages out of *Winnie the Pooh*, his favorite book. And I explained the meaning behind the pages—his meaning as best as I could imagine it to be. I shared the irony of a tough military colonel who was sensitive enough to proclaim his favorite literary work to be a classic children's book. I talked about the healing that maybe hadn't happened in life with his loved ones with the hopes I felt he had that forgiveness could take place upon his death.

I brought this challenging and reclusive man to a new light right before his family's eyes. And when it was over, the armor they had been wearing in the beginning had all been replaced with tears and love. They were able to let go of the hostility, disappointments, resentment, and maybe even some guilt as we laid their father to rest.

Following the ceremony, the children came up to me in tears and said, "How did you do that? How did you move us? How did you make us feel things we hadn't felt about him in so many years?" I simply responded with the truth and said, "Because, I told HIS story and made today, THIS day, all about him."

What I am trying to share is several things. One, that a great funeral can be done for anyone because everyone is unique in his or her own way—even if we don't understand it. Two, that a funeral has the ability to heal those who are there seeking restoration and closure. The finality of death encourages a time for allowing bygones to be bygones and inspires a sense of moving on from a past that may have harbored ill feelings. And three, a funeral is a tribute to the life you have lived. An honor of you. A chance for everyone to know what you have done, how you have lived, and who you have been.

I assure you, if I was able to turn that first funeral into something that changed the family's entire demeanor and mindset, then you can plan an amazing funeral for yourself!

Funeral Decisions and Details

I imagine the first thing that comes to people's minds when they think about funeral decisions is, "cremation or burial"? So, let's begin with that topic. I like to revert to basic definitions when we are discussing important matters in this book. Therefore, while most of us know the difference between a cremation and a burial, let's explore both.

A cremation is defined as reducing a dead body to ashes by fire, especially as a funeral rite.

A burial is defined as the act of burying, the interment of a dead body to include the burial place, tomb or final resting location.

Each process typically involves a ceremony, memorial, or tribute often referred to as a funeral for the deceased individual. Please note that the specific definitions of "funeral service" and "memorial service" are different. A funeral service typically involves the services of a funeral home and usually takes place at a funeral home, church, temple, or synagogue. The definitive difference is that at a funeral service, the deceased body is present in some form, and this service typically takes place quickly following the individual's death.

A memorial service is not typically in the presence of the body of the person who has passed and can be held anywhere and at any time, since typically no "body" is involved; however, quite often the ashes are present. This approach allows a lot of flexibility in honoring the passing of the individual. Please note for the sake of this section and the subject we are covering, I use the terms funeral service and memorial service interchangeably and I am intending them as a unified meaning of your final tribute and memorial to you. It is also important to note that in some parts of the country this tribute is called a celebration of life.

This is where your planning can become quite creative, since this portion is not dealing with how to handle your physical body, but instead with how to pay tribute to the human aspect of our lives. A funeral is often held at the funeral home. However, there can be graveside services, church tributes and services, and an array of other venues to offer a loving tribute to the deceased individual. Your funeral can be anywhere you want it to be. It can be at your peaceful place, the beach, your church, the lake, your back yard, a theater—limited only by your imagination.

I do want to address those unexpected and unplanned funerals because they do exist in large numbers, and in those situations, one must do the best he or she can with the circumstances presented.

I recently received a call from a friend whose father is on hospice, and they were expecting his passing very soon. The father had been suffering from Alzheimer's for quite some time, and it was evident that his body was shutting down. The arrangements for this gentleman had been prepaid a little over a year ago, as this issue became the focus of the family's life. However, the dynamics of this situation involve a geographically scattered relative base. There is one remaining sister in Indiana. There is his wife who resides in an assisted living facility in the same town as he does who does not want to make any decisions or face that the death of her husband is imminent, so she remains in denial. There are grown children displaced throughout Florida. And there is one son living locally, who has handled the bulk of all of these affairs.

The son who resides locally contacted me and asked me what he should do, feeling that the brunt of this issue was left to him. He knew his father wanted to be cremated, and they had paid for that. He just did not know what to do from there. He stated that there was really nobody left to come to his funeral because his social circle at this stage of life was quite small and those few individuals were displaced. I explained to him that it was not necessary for him to have a traditional funeral and suggested that the few individuals who wanted to pay tribute could meet at the cemetery and hold their own meaningful and private farewell prior to him being placed in his slot or drawer that had been pre-arranged.

He then stated that his father was not going to a cemetery and that his ashes were going in a box and would be given to a family member. This certainly did create some challenges as to where and how to pay some form of tribute to his father. He later revealed that his mother wanted the father's ashes to be spread over the grave of their daughter, who had passed in utero over four decades ago. However, the glitch was that she wanted her ashes intertwined with his and wanted them sprinkled together, which meant everyone had to wait for her to die to carry out this last wish.

Each new detail unfolded more challenges for this gentleman's farewell. I told the son that the burden did not have to fall on him and him alone.

While sometimes opening the floor to other perspectives creates even more complicated choices, I felt he needed to do two things. First, he needed to contact his father's elderly sister who resided in Indiana. I said this because he stated that this sister would need closure, and the challenge was that a trip to Florida could be a genuine hardship both physically and financially on her. Waiting to spread the ashes upon his mother's death did not guarantee that the sister would still be alive to take part in that event. So I advised him to have a discussion with her about what she felt she could and would do and what kind of closure she would need to accept and heal from the passing of her final remaining sibling.

Second, I advised him to contact his three siblings. They resided on the west coast of Florida and had been down the week prior per his prompting that they probably should seize the opportunity for a final farewell to their father. He told me he was not sure they would come to the funeral because they had just made the trip to see him. I told him that instead of assuming what their actions would be when their father passed, he should contact them to ask them their plans. I felt he needed to receive their input as to how their father should be laid to rest upon his passing. Then, upon gathering the various details, they could formulate a plan from there.

In cases where no funeral plans have been made it is challenging to even negotiate a farewell. This situation is not uncommon. As we age, our collective circle that might have started out as quite large, shrinks. While no funeral plans had been made for this gentleman and Alzheimer's had evaporated his friendship base a long time ago, there seemed to be few remaining people left to say goodbye. Even had a funeral been planned in great detail, it may not have unfolded as originally envisioned, as the best of plans can be eradicated due to the reality of life interrupted.

Obviously, this book is about planning, so the situation I just revealed could leave you wondering, "Then why plan at all if in the end it is all going to fall apart?" My answer is simply, "Because while your life may change the plans you have in place, some of them can still be executed on your behalf, and the family will have some form of meaningful details inspired by you." If this same gentleman had completed this book and had his funeral laid out in meticulous detail and had certain requests such as a release of 100 brightly colored balloons for all of his funeral patrons to enjoy releasing as a tribute to his passing, then that component could still be carried out by the few family members left. They could get the balloons, perhaps only a dozen, and release them in the parking lot of the funeral home as they held hands and said a loving farewell. Believe it or not, this would be some kind of closure for them because they had some personal touches that they knew meant something to their father.

In this particular situation I have shared, everyone is lost. They have no idea what he would have wanted. They are not organized at all. They do not even know what to do with the box of ashes when the funeral home gives it to them. If he put in writing, "I want my son to maintain my ashes until my wife passes and the final tribute can be carried out," they would be released from this decision. A plan provides the survivors with some kind of road map with which to navigate your passing. Even if much of it is not applicable due to the circumstances of your life, at least there is something in writing that your survivors can use to make the decisions as to what can be incorporated and what is not applicable. In the end, your plan is helpful, regardless.

As to the situation of this gentleman who contacted me, he is scurrying to race the clock and get something figured out before his father dies. My hopes are that with family input, they can create some type of recognition or acknowledgment on their loved one's behalf that will allow everyone to experience closure. I have shared this story to shed light on the stress and frustration involved when there is no plan at all.

If you are planning to have your funeral service at the funeral home, many of the arrangements are typically carried out by the funeral home director and staff. They are very skilled at ensuring a smooth funeral service and can accomplish such tasks as printing out your memorial handouts, collecting information to publish the obituary, and executing all aspects of the funeral procession.

Having said that, when you put your wishes in writing with regard to your expectations for your own funeral, you may dictate how you wish for this event to unfold. Be creative! Why be normal? This is a moment to really consider how you can leave a lasting impression on those who love and care about you. If you can think of it, or if it is meaningful, feel free to be bold enough to incorporate it.

Your funeral can be serious and somber
or it can be an all-out party!

If you are seeking that party funeral effect, imagine this. If you are a lady who appreciates a good-looking man, do you want Chippendales look-a-likes to be your pall bearers? Imagine eight shirtless, muscular men in tuxedo pants and all abs carrying you to your final resting place as the song "It's Raining Men" plays loudly in the background! I guess many of your female guests would replace a few of those crocodile tears with awe, admiration and, best of all, laughter. Offensive tribute to some? Maybe. But why do you care since you won't be too concerned with other people's opinion at the time. Will it be memorable? Yes! I speculate it will be unforgettable!

Are you into super heroes? Imagine mandating that mourners dress up as their favorite super hero to attend your funeral, as one final and lasting tribute to you! Are you a dancer? How about a fun and lively graveside Macarena in your honor? Did you throw yourself into support and volunteerism at the SPCA? Request every adoptable dog be sitting adorably in the pews and solicit one final tribute to your devoted cause. Implore your funeral guests to take one of those dogs home in honor of you! (Talk about a final guilt card!) Or if you are not feeling that bold, ask them to leave making a donation to your cause in your name.

Do you see where I am going with this? The word FUN is in the word FUNeral. So be sure you are thinking about yourself, who you have been, what you have loved, and how you have lived, when you are planning your FUNeral. If you have always been outgoing, or the life of the party, you may want to go out that way too!

Here is the test to find whether your
mission on earth is finished.
If you're alive, it isn't.
~RICHARD BACH

For those of you who haven't enjoyed the limelight and have lived on the more reserved side, you will want to go a different route and probably want no part of the aforementioned antics. But, that is fine because it is who you are. You may want specific poems, book passages, or Biblical verses read, or songs or hymns sung. Your funeral can be a great time of genuine reflection. Give some thought as to what you envision because this is a very important aspect of your peaceful passing and life celebration.

My father passed away just prior to the final edits of this book. And, because I write and officiate funerals, my family asked that I compose and deliver his funeral eulogy. So, I felt compelled to include it in this section. My father was a genuinely unique individual (understating), and I most definitely wanted his funeral to reflect the person HE was. Not necessarily the person society (or even I) may have always wanted him to be. He was a non-conforming, reclusive, brilliant man who lived life on his terms. That didn't always work out the best for those who loved him. But, we did love him, in spite of him. And, I made sure that I did not let him down in his death.

I wrote a service for him that he would have loved! While I provided a factual overview and account of his life and lineage, and professional accomplishments, I told attendees to "brace yourselves for a non-traditional tribute to an unconventional man." This service was in no way normal, but neither was he. My eulogy referenced some abbreviated profanity. To say my father had a "potty mouth" was a colossal understatement. This was done to illustrate some of his favorite words and how he "eloquently" and creatively used them. While I heard an incredible amount of laughter at this, I am quite confident it was equally matched with shock value, yet another component of this funeral that my father would have relished. I summarized that subject with, "I'm sorry if that offended some of you. But, if it did, you probably didn't know my father very well."

I shared his many passions and loves, and I shared my idolization of him from when I was young. I credited him for teaching me how to ride horses, perhaps not equestrian school style, but I sure learned how to ride. I shared some truly funny stories that involved some questionable circumstances and activities in his life. He was passionate about reptiles, and the opening song I chose to play was one he loved, "Spiders and Snakes" by Jim Stafford. I would bet this song had never been played at a funeral before. But, this was my dad's day and my dad's music was going to be heard.

I also stated, "When asked to stand before you today, I didn't see my job as one to justify anything my dad had ever done, or even worse—to tell you he was someone he really wasn't." There is no doubt that I verbally illuminated my dad, and people had no choice but to admire and embrace the man I disclosed—good, bad and indifferent. In fact, they just respected him for being a rebel, being his own man, and truly not caring about conformity. I heard laughter, witnessed tears, but most of all provided undeniable clarity and acceptance of who he really was. In other words, I honored him as the person HE was. Afterwards, people came up to me and admitted that they had no idea what to expect when they heard the "Spiders and Snakes" song. Some people told me it was one of the most incredible services they had ever attended. They stated that after hearing the many stories about him, they understood him better than they ever had before. It was as if they had a new appreciation for him. It seems for some people, I had provided a voice of clarity for my dad in death that he had been unable to articulate for himself while living.

While I had been honest in each word I spoke, my goal was to serve as a gateway from his grave to the mourners that came to pay respect. I used my voice to channel the best and truest essence of him, while keeping it real. I conveyed this message as I believe he would have wanted, recognizing that he wouldn't and couldn't have said these things himself, even if he were alive.

A funeral shouldn't just be about what the world wants to hear. A funeral should be highly personal and reflect the greatest aspects of our living, our unique character, ourselves. No, we're not perfect. We all could afford a "do-over" on certain things. Certainly not everyone that dies is considered "wonderfully amazing" or a "catastrophic loss" by surviving society at large. However, there is good to uncover in every life. It may require a little polish, perhaps dusting off, straightening of our halo or even a magnifying spot light to uncover our most amazing traits—but it is there and should be shared and honored.

I have given you some non-typical considerations earlier in this section. But, blaze your own trail that speaks to the person you are. Traditional or non-traditional is perfectly fine, as long as it is what you personally desire.

I have been to funerals that have incorporated many unique aspects. I recall one in which the individual had an early passing with the unfortunate fate of dying from ovarian cancer. The family was devastated, needless to say. However, they believed that this life was a transition into the next phase of our immortal spirit and believed that the dying experience was merely a transformation into immortality.

With this concept, they ordered hundreds of butterflies to be released following the service to emulate the rebirth experience through the symbolism of the butterflies' metamorphosis. Each individual was given a butterfly pod that housed a beautiful butterfly, and they were released simultaneously as the family shouted "Farewell" to their loved one. This moment stood still with reflection as laughter, tears, and silence were all transpiring simultaneously. It was both heartfelt and meaningful and portrayed the individual in the manner that I believe she would have greatly appreciated. But releasing the butterflies was more than that; it allowed a means for acceptance of her young passing so healing could follow.

Nothing is off limits. So I ask you to consider who you are and what matters to you. Some have been buried with a bottle of Jack Daniels, clearly their beverage of choice in their life time. Others have had their own unique twist on the dying experience. They have asked to be buried faced down, with food and money, with their beloved pet's ashes. I recently heard of someone who wanted to be in his open casket; and instead of it being placed horizontal, he wished to be staged in a vertical position. He felt he was vertical in life and he wanted people to come up and look him eye to eye and say farewell rather than looking down upon his body in a sleeping state.

So, what are you thinking? Do you have any ideas? If not, it's okay because we will do some worksheets to help you formulate ideas of your own that are relevant to you. Just remember, as I have been saying, in our life a lot has gone into every detail of your celebrated occasions such as birthdays, anniversaries, and special parties. Don't slight yourself by missing the opportunity to make your final farewell memorable and amazing.

While I thought
that I was learning how to live,
I have been learning how to die.
~LEONARDO DA VINCI

You now have the inspiration to get pretty creative with your actual funeral service. With the worksheets to follow, you can devise your funeral plan. So let's go back and discuss topics related to both cremation and burials. Yes, you should pick a preference in regard to these options. This will save your family from trying to choose a preference for you. First, though, I must mention the following, as this book is about offering you information as it relates to these topics. There are more choices than just cremation or casket. You would be surprised as to the many different forms of burial today. Let's explore a few of them to allow you the opportunity to make your best choice.

Non-Traditional Burial Options

How about being launched into outer space and orbiting in the atmosphere until the end of time? It's really possible! Visit my website to find out more about non-traditional burial options. Including, how some of your cremated remains can be launched into the galaxy, if you so desire! Talk about an explosive exit! How about being frozen forever in time? How about a green burial in which your body is swaddled in earth-friendly, biodegradable materials and there is no casket or typical enclosure to house your remains? Do any of these options appeal to you? Well, non-customary burial options are in abundance. So, here's a little information on some less traditional approaches to the burial process.

I won't go into great detail here for the sake of simplicity. I only want you to know that alternatives exist, so that you may further explore them if this is something that interests you. I could write an entire book on just non-traditional burials, and some people have done so already. My goal is just to create awareness of various options. This book is a general overview of the topics herein. We are only scratching the surface, and honestly, I feel if we went much deeper, many of you would put the book down and not do what is most important overall from this mission, and that is to get your planning done. Much of what we cover here is simple and generalized. But I urge you that if any of it is not detailed enough, perform further research before making your final plans in those areas.

Non-traditional burial options are becoming more popular. Consider these facts below regarding the traditional burial statistics.

As the ecological impact of a traditional burial is understood, individuals are considering the impact on the environment. For instance, did you know each year, 22,500 cemeteries across the United States bury approximately:

~ embalming fluid: 827,060 gallons, which includes formaldehyde

~ caskets: 90,000 tons of steel

~ caskets: 2,700 tons of copper and bronze

~ caskets: 30-plus million board feet of hardwoods

~ vaults: 1.6 million tons of reinforced concrete

~ vaults: 14,000 tons of steel

Compiled from statistics by Casket and Funeral Association of America, Cremation Association of North America, Doric Inc., The Rainforest Action Network, and Mary Woodsen, Pre-Posthumous Society, Science Researcher, Writer for Cornell University, Founding President Greensprings Natural Cemetery.

Green Burials

Green burials, or natural burials, are becoming more popular as more and more people begin to share concern for our environmental state. Such burials, however, are not available just anywhere. Though more and more burial grounds are beginning to recognize the desire for such options, you will need to do some checking around to explore the locations where this is available. The internet, as I have mentioned previously, will open up many options for you when you perform your basic search on the topics we review in this book.

Overall, a green burial excludes the use of chemicals and preservatives and does not include any metals, concrete, or other non-green friendly materials in the process of the burial. This is a very natural process of decomposition, which involves no embalming fluids, rare woods, or plastic materials. Instead, your remains are placed in a paper, cardboard, or non-treated wood enclosure, or even a biodegradable fabric of your choosing.

While we are calling this type of burial non-traditional and considering it a "newer" burial option, please keep in mind that what goes around comes around. What I am saying is the same thing my mother always told me: "Keep that even though it is outdated. It will come back into style one day!" Well, it wasn't long ago that most of our ancestors' funerals involved what we now term as a "green" or "natural" burial.

While embalming and other preserving measures of dealing with a corpse have been utilized for centuries in some areas of the globe, many burials hundreds of years ago were simply a body placed in the ground or in a basic container. And since I am on this subject, embalming is an option in many instances. There are situations where it is necessary to embalm, but please know that it is not always a mandate, and is a decision you may be left to make.

Other Non-Traditional Burial Options

I won't cover these options in great detail. But, I will mention them for your awareness and enlightenment (and in some cases, entertainment).

~ Cremated remains launched into space

~ Burial at sea

~ Reef burials and underwater cemeteries

~ Mummification

~ Plastination

~ Cryogenic freezing

~ Organ and tissue donation

~ Scientific donation

~ Alternate cremation

~ Diamonds are forever

~ Memorial work of art

And the list goes on. A quick search of any of these options will offer more detailed information on the process and costs. There are a variety of companies offering these and other burial alternatives. New ways of dealing with remains are emerging all of the time, compliments of the inventive and creative world we live in. If any of these types of alternatives peak your interest, definitely search this subject matter to see what you find most fitting to your specific preferences, and also visit my website to learn about new and innovative options that I might be sharing.

A man's dying

is more

the survivors' affair

than his own.

~THOMAS MANN

Your Funeral and Burial Preferences

There are many decisions to make regarding your final passing. If you wish to be buried in a casket, which type do you want? What will you be wearing? Have you ever said, "I wouldn't be caught dead wearing THAT?" Well, be careful what you say. In other words, make sure you aren't wearing such an outfit on your final day! That is why we are putting your planning in writing. And, just in case, I would suggest throwing out any hideous fashion disasters you may have lurking in your closet to avoid any confusion! How do you want your hair and makeup? Open or closed casket? But, as you will see, these are questions for you to answer in your workbook pages. And, I would rather spend more time with you in our question and answer session than having you read about things you probably already have worked out.

Therefore, I just want to move on to some of the many questions that you need to respond to regarding your burial and funeral, and I believe you are ready to do this. The following workbook pages will allow you to plan and finalize the many details regarding your burial or cremation. Please note that we are covering the details of your BURIAL/CREMATION workbook pages first. Following that, we will explore the specifics of your FUNERAL or MEMORIAL SERVICE. Even though they are typically done together in the same day, they are two different facets of your funeral.

I wake up every morning at
nine and grab for the
morning paper.
Then I look at the
obituary page.
If my name is not on it,
I get up.
~BENJAMIN FRANKLIN

WORKBOOK PAGES
BURIAL/CREMATION

☐ Check here if you have already planned your funeral with a funeral home.

Which funeral home? _____

    (Please place papers/contract the separate notebook you have made)

☐ Check here if you have pre-paid for your funeral and burial

Which funeral home? _____

    (Please place papers/contract in the separate notebook you have made)

☐ Check here if you have a burial plot, cremation drawer or location, a crypt or mausoleum already purchased.

    (Please place papers/contact in the separate notebook you have made)

☐ Check here if you have a final expense plan or burial plan, Totten Trust, or other type of life insurance policy. *(If yes, please make sure you log the details of it in the insurance section of this workbook and place related paperwork in your separate notebook)*

I wish to be:

        ☐ buried   ☐ cremated   ☐ OTHER (Explain below)

_____

_____

_____

_____

_____

_____

_____

_____

If you have chosen BURIAL, please list the type of casket you would prefer. *(Be specific, including such details as materials, colors, themes, inscriptions, pictures or drawings—caskets are a huge industry, and they are available in just about any fashion, material, or style you would prefer. Caskets can even be purchased online such as at AMAZON, Costco, and other major retailers. Caskets today are highly individualized if you wish to buy one. If you already have, put the details of that purchase here and paperwork in your separate notebook.)*

Do you want an open or closed casket?

☐ Open   ☐ Closed

Any specific rituals or wishes you have regarding your casket?

_____

_____

_____

_____

_____

_____

Is there anything you want placed inside your casket with you? (Explain)

_____

_____

_____

_____

_____

What clothing do you want to wear in your casket? (Be specific)

_____

_____

_____

_____

_____

How do you want your hair and make-up, if you wish to have an open casket?

_____

_____

Is there anyone in particular that you have designated to do your hair and make-up? *(Note: Funeral homes often have professional mortuary make-up artists)*

☐ Yes   ☐ No

If yes, provide name and phone number:

_____

_____

☐ I would like the funeral home to handle this procedure.

Do you wish to have a separate viewing or visitation hours in addition to your funeral service viewing?

☐ Yes   ☐ No

If you are choosing cremation, have you chosen a container or urn?

☐ Yes   ☐ No

If yes, describe:

_____

_____

_____

_____

If no, what ideas do you have regarding selection? (Describe)

_____

_____

_____

_____

What are your preferences if you have not yet chosen an urn?

_____

_____

_____

_____

What are your wishes for your cremated remains? Do you want them scattered or kept with a family member? Do you want them in a vault, a drawer, or buried? Other preferences? Please explain in detail:

_____

_____

_____

_____

_____

_____

_____

_____

What is/are your favorite flower(s)?

_____

_____

_____

Do you want flowers at your ceremony?

☐ Yes   ☐ No

If no, is there something you want in lieu of flowers, such as donations to an organization, etc.? Explain:

_____

_____

_____

_____

_____

If you are choosing a burial, what type of grave marker would you prefer? (Choices are abundant and may include a headstone either flat or upright, a bench, a sculpture, etc.)

_____

_____

_____

If you are choosing a burial, how do you want your grave marker to read? (Typically a grave marker includes personal information such as the full name of the deceased, date of birth, date of death, and some words of sentiment regarding the individual or even a short written memorial tribute to them.)

_____

_____

_____

_____

_____

Where do you want your casket or urn to be placed? (Your choices are abundant but include a crypt, a drawer, mausoleum, etc.)

A crypt is a larger area comprised of heavy-duty construction. It allows room for caskets or urns and is typically ideal for storage of multiple family members and loved ones in one location.

A drawer is a slot specifically designed to hold the cremated remains of the deceased. Typically, these slots are often arranged in rows both vertical and horizontal. Once the remains are placed in them, the slots are permanently sealed.

A mausoleum is above ground and often quite large and grand. They are obviously more costly than the other options outlined and are typically intended to accommodate multiple loved ones together inside.

☐ crypt   ☐ drawer   ☐ mausoleum   ☐ OTHER (describe below)

_____

_____

_____

_____

If you are choosing a means of multiple storage, such as a crypt or mausoleum, who else do you wish to be joining you upon their passing?

_____

_____

_____

If choosing burial, do you wish to have pall bearers? If so, whom?

_____

_____

_____

ANY other details you wish to add regarding your...

Burial or Cremation:

_____

_____

_____

Casket or Urn or other:

_____

_____

_____

Final resting place:

_____

_____

_____

Other specifics:

_____

_____

_____

_____

YOUR Funeral and Ceremony

Your ceremony is one of the most important aspects of your funeral. Your burial—well that is mostly for you and suitable to your preferences. But your funeral ceremony or memorial, that is for those you are leaving behind. And I know you see the value in why that portion of your passing is so very important.

Your ceremony should represent your personal vision of how you want it to go. Think about the funerals you have been to and consider what worked for some and made them meaningful; and at the same time, reflect back on the funerals you have been to that incorporated few personal touches and were simply a ritual being obliged. We've shared some unique ways to make ceremonies special. Now it is time to put some of your own ideas into writing. Let's get started on planning your funeral service tribute.

When you were born,

you cried

and the world rejoiced.

Live your life

so that when you die,

the world cries and you rejoice.

~CHEROKEE EXPRESSION

YOUR FUNERAL SERVICE
WORKBOOK PLANNING PAGES

Just to get started, begin to visualize your funeral or memorial service in your mind. Is it at a funeral home? Is it grave side? Is it serious? Is it funny? Is it a show? Or is it a solemn and meaningful remembrance of you?

In the space below, quickly pencil out some quick notes as to how you envision your funeral service. (Note, we will do a specific plan following. This exercise is just to get your basic thoughts down.)

_____
_____
_____
_____
_____
_____
_____
_____
_____
_____
_____
_____
_____
_____
_____
_____
_____
_____
_____
_____
_____
_____

Okay, let's discuss all the different components that go into the orchestration of your funeral service.

I have given you some outlandish ideas, creative concepts, as well as some simple tributes that will allow you to have the funeral service of your choosing. You will use the workbook pages to make selections of personal preferences, including your favorite songs, poems, and other special details you wish to incorporate.

In the separate binder you've created, I encourage you to place any poems or songs that you may have listed, so that your family members may easily obtain them and begin orchestrating your service when the time arises. The more you give them here, the easier their job is at the time.

In this section, complete as much as you choose. You may not know some answers or wish to leave the final details up to those who will be handling this matter, but provide as much information as you feel is important to help them accomplish that task.

First things first. Imagine you have just died. There is something to be done first and foremost. Do you know what that important detail is? There is one detail we don't want to overlook. It will be important to tell others of your unfortunate passing. You have an intimate circle of friends and relatives. Of course, you will want each person notified immediately. But, think about your life and daily or weekly activities. Who do you associate with that your loved ones may potentially miss due to lack of awareness?

Are you a member of the senior center? Do you lead a cause? Are you a member of Pilot Club? Rotary? Kiwanis? Do you volunteer at Hospice or the hospital? Do you deliver Meals on Wheels? Are you a member of a church or part of a prayer group?

Think of everything you do in your life and consider the people you come into contact with including long-time friends you rarely see but who have always been special to you. The organizations and people you know also need to be notified of your passing. Your work colleagues or former coworkers, your high school and college friends, the list goes on. Throughout your life, you have known a lot of people, some of whom remain very special to you. They would want to know of course, but they also need to know. Much of your life is just that, YOUR life. So, your family may not know of the detailed notifications which would need to be done outside of your close network of friends and family.

In the space below, please make a list of the people who would need to be notified about your passing. The first list is a quick name/number reference for professional contacts, known family and close friends, and those to be contacted first. The sheets thereafter are for extended friends, club associates, and acquaintances; they require more detail so your family will know how you have come to know them.

IN THE EVENT OF MY DEATH, THE FIRST PEOPLE TO CONTACT ARE:

Name: (Family/Friend)   Address: Phone:

_____   Employer   _____

_____   Stockbroker   _____

_____   Attorney   _____

_____   Insurance Broker   _____

_____   Accountant/CPA   _____

_____   Funeral Home   _____

_____

_____

_____

_____

_____

_____

_____

_____

_____

_____

_____

_____

_____

_____

_____

_____

IN THE EVENT OF MY DEATH, THE FOLLOWING PEOPLE SHOULD ALSO BE NOTIFIED:

Name: _____Phone: _____

Relationship or Association: _____

Other: (address, e-mail or details) _____

Name: _____Phone: _____

Relationship or Association: _____

Other: (address, e-mail or details) _____

Name: _____Phone: _____

Relationship or Association: _____

Other: (address, e-mail or details) _____

Name: _____Phone: _____

Relationship or Association: _____

Other: (address, e-mail or details) _____

Name: _____Phone: _____

Relationship or Association: _____

Other: (address, e-mail or details) _____

Name: _____Phone: _____

Relationship or Association: _____

Other: (address, e-mail or details) _____

Name: _____Phone: _____

Relationship or Association: _____

Other: (address, e-mail or details) _____

Name: _____Phone: _____

Relationship or Association: _____

Other: (address, e-mail or details) _____

Name: _____Phone: _____

Relationship or Association: _____

Other: (address, e-mail or details) _____

Name: _____Phone: _____

Relationship or Association: _____

Other: (address, e-mail or details) _____

Name: _____Phone: _____

Relationship or Association: _____

Other: (address, e-mail or details) _____

Name: _____Phone: _____

Relationship or Association: _____

Other: (address, e-mail or details) _____

Name: _____Phone: _____

Relationship or Association: _____

Other: (address, e-mail or details) _____

Name: _____Phone: _____

Relationship or Association: _____

Other: (address, e-mail or details) _____

(If additional space is needed make a section for this in your separate notebook)

Typically, the funeral home will prepare a memorial handout for the deceased. This includes the basic details of his or her life: date of birth, date of death, full name, and maybe even a special short poem or favorite Biblical verse. It usually includes a photograph on the front with the birth and death dates listed underneath. It will highlight the funeral or memorial agenda of the ceremony and list the officiator(s). What would you like your funeral memorial to include? You can write it in its entirety or offer a few ideas.

_____
_____
_____
_____
_____
_____
_____
_____
_____
_____
_____
_____
_____
_____
_____
_____
_____
_____
_____
_____
_____
_____
_____
_____

Where do you want this service to take place? (Funeral home, beach, graveside, church, synagogue, temple, home, park, etc., specifically describe.)

_____

_____

_____

If you are a member or have a church preference, please list below:

_____

_____

_____

What are your religious or spiritual beliefs (if any)?

_____

_____

_____

What religion are you (if applicable)?

_____

_____

_____

If possible, do you prefer to incorporate some customs into your ceremony related to your religious or cultural beliefs?

☐ Yes   ☐ No

If yes, explain:

_____

_____

_____

_____

_____

_____

Do you have a music selection you would like playing as guests enter and wait for the ceremony to begin? Is it a recording, someone singing live, etc.? (Be specific and if no preference, state so.)

_____

_____

_____

_____

_____

What other music do you want either performed or played during your funeral service? (List name of song and performer, if applicable. For music selections list song name and artist.)

_____

_____

_____

_____

_____

Who do you want to officiate or deliver your funeral service? (Pastor, Clergy, Rabbi, friend, relative, someone you've pre-selected, etc.)

_____

_____

_____

_____

Do you want someone to give a tribute at your funeral, such as read a poem or a portion of a book or Bible verse? If yes, please list whom and specifically what poem or verse:

_____

_____

_____

_____

_____

Often people close to the deceased will also speak and address the guests. Who, if anyone, would you like to do this? Is there any particular topic or story you want them to share, or do you just want them to create their own speech? (List preferences and please be specific if you are selecting a story or topic. This is a great time to consider special memories or funny stories that can really add a personal touch to your funeral and give your friends an opportunity to participate in sharing their relationship with you and honor you in a way that can promote healing and make your tribute meaningful and unique.)

_____
_____
_____
_____
_____
_____
_____
_____
_____
_____
_____
_____
_____
_____
_____
_____
_____
_____
_____
_____
_____
_____

Is there a message FROM YOU that you can create in the space below that you would like read aloud to the mourners at your funeral service? If so, read by whom? (Remember this is to a general audience. Your personal sentiments are contained in your "All About Me" section and "Letters to Loved Ones" section.)

Read by: _____

Message from you:

_____
_____
_____
_____
_____
_____
_____
_____
_____
_____
_____
_____
_____
_____
_____
_____
_____
_____
_____
_____
_____
_____
_____

Would you like a slide show depicting some of your life's most memorable times? If so, choose photos and set them aside in your separate notebook titled, "My funeral slide show photos" or "My Funeral Photos." Or, you can also simply compile the photos and they can be used to be made into a collage on a poster board by your loved ones.

I ☐ have ☐ have not set aside photos for a slide show or photo collage.

Is there a favorite quote you want to share on this day? (If so, write it below.)

_____

_____

_____

_____

_____

Do you have any parting advice you wish to share? (Remember this is to a general audience. You will have written your "Dear Loved Ones" and completed the "All About Me" pages which are devoted to special sentiments to loved ones.)

_____

_____

_____

_____

_____

_____

_____

_____

_____

_____

_____

I took the road less traveled by,
and that has made all the difference.
~ROBERT FROST

What special touches make your funeral ceremony unique?

We discussed this earlier with some FUN ideas as well as some highly personal and meaningful tributes, from the Chippendales pall bearers to the butterfly release! Ideas include blowing bubbles, having your dogs present, balloon release, fireworks, a rocket launching your cremains into outer space, a ceremonial tree planting, a unified toast with a shot of whiskey, something special on display, YOU displayed in a special manner! A candle-lighting ceremony, your family and friends each sharing a story or thoughts about you. Music that symbolizes who and what you are. Stories that invoke special moments of your life or even ones that are funny or hilarious. The list goes on and on. The choices are limitless! Be creative! Explain:

What will be unique about your funeral?

_____

_____

_____

_____

_____

_____

_____

_____

_____

_____

_____

_____

_____

_____

_____

_____

_____

_____

_____

Is there anything else not captured previously that you wish to add or incorporate into your funeral service? (Please be specific.)

_____

_____

_____

_____

_____

_____

_____

_____

_____

_____

_____

_____

_____

_____

_____

_____

_____

_____

_____

_____

_____

_____

_____

_____

_____

_____

_____

_____

_____

_____

Wow! Do you know that you just planned your own funeral? I cannot believe it! I hope you are smiling, because I am! I am excited as I consider all the many different ways that each reader put their fingerprint on their own farewell! I know you have made your funeral unique, interesting, meaningful, and perhaps even a little fun. You have handled something very important not only for yourself but for those you love! Congratulations! You have just completed the "YOUR Funeral" section of this book and YOUR funeral is planned!

Give sorrow words;

the grief that does not speak

Knits up the o-er wrought heart

and bids it break.

~WILLIAM SHAKESPEARE, MACBETH

CHAPTER 13

The Nitty-Gritty Deets!

It's All in the Details!

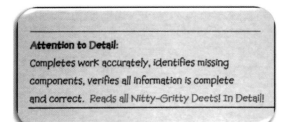

Attention to Detail:
Completes work accurately, identifies missing components, verifies all information is complete and correct. Reads all Nitty-Gritty Deets! In Detail!

In this chapter, you will list of all of your personal and business-related matters and then some! If you take your time and complete this chapter in its entirety, there will be little left to the imagination. Having said that, there is a significant amount of private and sensitive information here as well. My suggestion remains to keep this book in a place where it is safe and private. Many people have a small fire box or safe. That is a great place to keep YOUR book as long as someone close to you knows that it exists and knows how to access the box or safe.

Don't let this chapter intimidate you. It contains a lot of sections, but you can get through this quickly once you get started. Also, it is intended to appeal to a vast readership and therefore only certain areas will pertain to each person.

And remember, at the end of this chapter you will find a section titled "Everything and Anything Else." This is for any item you may have or need to share, that may not have been captured in the pages provided. Please include those items in that section. Without further ado, let's get started!

We don't stop playing because we grow old;

We grow old because we stop playing.

~GEORGE BERNARD SHAW

Personal Accounts

We all have a lot of different accounts these days, credited to the modern computer era, shopping sites, and even social media. Many people have personal and professional e-mail accounts, eBay accounts, Amazon accounts, Facebook and Twitter accounts, iTunes accounts, etc. I would speculate that when you begin brainstorming, you will have more accounts than you realize.

This is NOT the section to list your credit card accounts as there is an area in this book designated for that type of financial information. In this section, list the various personal or professional accounts you access and utilize. **Remember, maintain your passwords in a separate notebook that is kept in a safe location.**

In this section, list your account(s) and user names so that in the event they would need to be discontinued, the information regarding which account you have is available.

Under "OTHER DETAILS" at the end of each form, please include information such as credits you may have, a gift card, a pre-paid offer, or other relevant details associated with that account.

USER ACCOUNT LOG

Account with: _____

Web address to access account: _____

Other details regarding this account: _____

Account with: _____

Web address to access account: _____

Other details regarding this account: _____

Account with: _____

Web address to access account: _____

Other details regarding this account: _____

Account with: _____

Web address to access account: _____

Other details regarding this account: _____

Account with: _____

Web address to access account: _____

Other details regarding this account: _____

Account with: _____

Web address to access account: _____

Other details regarding this account: _____

Account with: _____

Web address to access account: _____

Other details regarding this account: _____

Safety Deposit Boxes, Safes, Vaults

If you have a safety deposit box, please include institution information below. It is important that someone you trust be made aware of the location of the box and key to be able to access this box. If you have a safe with a code or password, the same applies. However, I would discourage you from keeping the key and passwords in this book.

Regarding safety deposit boxes, **title of ownership determines who has access to this box.** Make sure you have this established properly with your financial institution so the person you designate can retrieve the contents. Otherwise, if there is sole ownership, more challenges will be encountered in the event of your death which will further complicate this matter.

One of the tragic things I know about human nature
is that all of us tend to put off living.
We are all dreaming of
some magical rose garden over the horizon—
instead of enjoying the roses that are blooming
outside our windows today.
~DALE CARNEGIE

SAFE BOX INFORMATION

Location: _____

Address : _____

Phone: _____

Person who knows how to access this box: _____

Location: _____

Address : _____

Phone: _____

Person who knows how to access this box: _____

Location: _____

Address : _____

Phone: _____

Person who knows how to access this box: _____

Location: _____

Address : _____

Phone: _____

Person who knows how to access this box: _____

Location: _____

Address : _____

Phone: _____

Person who knows how to access this box: _____

Finances

Your finances involve any banking accounts, savings, checking, money market, trust accounts, stocks/bonds, mutual funds, certificates of deposit, annuities, investments, and even money you may have hidden in your freezer or mattress (though I don't recommend it).

Please use the following spaces to list your financial accounts so that you have a comprehensive log covering all aspects of your financial endeavors. You will only list the general account details. As stated, **you will maintain confidential details in your separate notebook that you keep in a safe place.**

This is not the place to list credit cards. There is a dedicated section for that to follow. It is important to know that regarding stocks, bonds, and other funds, your stockbroker will proceed with appropriate transfers based on the title of ownership for each financial instrument and as it relates to the written wishes stipulated in your will or trust.

The safe way to double your money

is to fold it over once

and put it in your pocket.

~FRANK HUBBARD

In your separate notebook, maintain a current list of stocks, bonds, mutual and money market funds, and/or commodities, as well as list the number of shares, purchase date and price, and contact information for your brokerage firm, if applicable. In the section you have already completed, which was the "Who to call first in the event of my death," you will find "stockbroker" already listed there for your convenience and for you to finish the pertinent details.

For federally issued government bonds, your financial institution can assist you in redeeming these and provide information as to the required documentation needed to do so. Additionally, you may also visit the official Federal Reserve website for more information.

ACCOUNT(S) INFORMATION

*List the related information for these accounts such as account number, routing number, etc. in your separate notebook.

Type of Account:_____

Financial Institution Name:_____

Address:_____Phone:_____

Name of Advisor or Banking Representative:_____

Type of Account:_____

Financial Institution Name:_____

Address:_____Phone:_____

Name of Advisor or Banking Representative:_____

Type of Account:_____

Financial Institution Name:_____

Address:_____Phone:_____

Name of Advisor or Banking Representative:_____

Type of Account:_____

Financial Institution Name:_____

Address:_____Phone:_____

Name of Advisor or Banking Representative:_____

Type of Account:_____

Financial Institution Name:_____

Address:_____Phone:_____

Name of Advisor or Banking Representative:_____

Insurance Information

This section will allow you to log and provide details pertaining to your various insurance policies and coverage with each one. This will include any health insurance, life insurance, long-term care insurance, key man, personal property and homeowner's policies, supplemental policies such as Aflac or disability plans, travel and accident policies, automobile, and even burial insurance, credit card and bank-issued life insurance and accidental death policies.

Please try to capture all the various means by which you are insured. Some are easy to forget about if you have applied for the free policies offered through many banking institutions, and even some credit card companies offer life insurance as well. You may have insurance you purchase through work, or if you are retired, you may have a portability plan that you continue to maintain. This section will allow you to list all related coverage. If you work with an insurance broker, you can provide that information on the pages that follow.

How wonderful it is that nobody
need wait a single moment
before starting to improve the world.
~ANNE FRANK

INSURANCE INFORMATION

Insurer Name:_____

Address/Phone:_____

Contact or Agent/ Broker:_____

Type of policy:_____

How is it paid? (auto debit, check, etc.):_____

Mode of payment:_____

Insurer Name:_____

Address/Phone:_____

Contact or Agent/ Broker:_____

Type of policy:_____

How is it paid? (auto debit, check, etc.):_____

Mode of payment:_____

Insurer Name:_____

Address/Phone:_____

Contact or Agent/ Broker:_____

Type of policy:_____

How is it paid? (auto debit, check, etc.):_____

Mode of payment:_____

Insurer Name:_____

Address/Phone:_____

Contact or Agent/ Broker:_____

Type of policy:_____

How is it paid? (auto debit, check, etc.):_____

Mode of payment:_____

INSURANCE INFORMATION

Insurer Name:_____

Address/Phone:_____

Contact or Agent/ Broker:_____

Type of policy:_____

How is it paid? (auto debit, check, etc.):_____

Mode of payment:_____

Insurer Name:_____

Address/Phone:_____

Contact or Agent/ Broker:_____

Type of policy:_____

How is it paid? (auto debit, check, etc.):_____

Mode of payment:_____

Insurer Name:_____

Address/Phone:_____

Contact or Agent/ Broker:_____

Type of policy:_____

How is it paid? (auto debit, check, etc.):_____

Mode of payment:_____

Insurer Name:_____

Address/Phone:_____

Contact or Agent/ Broker:_____

Type of policy:_____

How is it paid? (auto debit, check, etc.):_____

Mode of payment:_____

Credit and Debit Card Information

Use this section to list all of your credit card companies, even those cards you don't use very often. So pull out your wallet and start archiving what you have. In the event the cards need to be canceled, this will be an easy way for the details to be accessed. **You will provide basic card information here, and put the actual card number in your separate notebook to maintain privacy.** While you are at it, please think of any store credits you may have, gift cards, Amazon credits, PayPal account credits and the like. You will want to uncover any means of credit pertaining to you!

Money can't buy you happiness
but it does bring you a
more pleasant form
of Misery.
~SPIKE MILLIGAN

CREDIT/DEBIT INFORMATION

Note: Be sure to log and maintain account number, expiration date, and security code in your separate notebook.

Name of Credit Card:_____

Is this a: ☐ store credit   ☐ credit card   ☐ debit card

Address/Phone:_____

Other details regarding this account (sky miles, points accrued, etc.):

_____

_____

_____

Name of Credit Card:_____

Is this a: ☐ store credit   ☐ credit card   ☐ debit card

Address/Phone:_____

Other details regarding this account (sky miles, points accrued, etc.):

_____

_____

_____

Name of Credit Card:_____

Is this a: ☐ store credit   ☐ credit card   ☐ debit card

Address/Phone:_____

Other details regarding this account (sky miles, points accrued, etc.):

_____

_____

_____

CREDIT/DEBIT INFORMATION

Note: Be sure to log and maintain account number, expiration date, and security code in your separate notebook.

Name of Credit Card:_____

Is this a: ☐ store credit   ☐ credit card   ☐ debit card

Address/Phone:_____

Other details regarding this account (sky miles, points accrued, etc.):

_____

_____

_____

Name of Credit Card:_____

Is this a: ☐ store credit   ☐ credit card   ☐ debit card

Address/Phone:_____

Other details regarding this account (sky miles, points accrued, etc.):

_____

_____

_____

Name of Credit Card:_____

Is this a: ☐ store credit   ☐ credit card   ☐ debit card

Address/Phone:_____

Other details regarding this account (sky miles, points accrued, etc.):

_____

_____

_____

CREDIT/DEBIT INFORMATION

Note: Be sure to log and maintain account number, expiration date, and security code in your separate notebook.

Name of Credit Card:_____

Is this a: ☐ store credit   ☐ credit card   ☐ debit card

Address/Phone:_____

Other details regarding this account (sky miles, points accrued, etc.):

_____

_____

_____

Name of Credit Card:_____

Is this a: ☐ store credit   ☐ credit card   ☐ debit card

Address/Phone:_____

Other details regarding this account (sky miles, points accrued, etc.):

_____

_____

_____

Name of Credit Card:_____

Is this a: ☐ store credit   ☐ credit card   ☐ debit card

Address/Phone:_____

Other details regarding this account (sky miles, points accrued, etc.):

_____

_____

_____

More forms available at www.sunriesandsunsetsbook.com

Personal Property

Personal Property is anything of either monetary or sentimental value. This is an area to include your prized possessions as well as family heirlooms you have been holding onto and preserving.

This area is included to allow you not only the opportunity to convey that the item exists in your possession, but it also allows you to write a little information as to why it is important (if that pertains). Sometimes, family members are unaware of the meaning of an item and may view it as insignificant unless you tell them the history and relevance of it.

What you don't want is for the antique treasure you have been holding onto throughout generations to end up in the estate garage sale selling for twenty dollars, only to be appraised on the Antique Road Show weeks later as half a million dollars! But, the items here do not have to have monetary value. Perhaps they are financially worth nothing but the sentimental value is priceless.

In my family, there is a small yet meaningful framed poem titled Mother's Love. It has no monetary value whatsoever. But, I am told it hung in my great grandmother's room when she was a young girl, and then my grandmother's room, my mother's room, then mine and I have given it to my daughter. It reads, "A Mother's Love is like a star that shines above both near and far. Though clouds may dim its light so fair, yet all the time the star is there." I hope this continues to be passed down in my family for generations to come.

Make sure you remember all those special things you have saved for the sake of passing on and continuing in the family legacy and log them in this section. **Note that archiving items in this section does not replace the need for designating personal property allocations in your will.**

PERSONAL PROPERTY ARCHIVE

Item: _____

Located:_____

Origin: _____

Meaning or Value:_____

Is there anyone special you would like to have this item   ☐ Yes   ☐ No

If so, whom:_____

What are your hopes regarding this item: _____

Why has this been special for you:_____

Other comments:

_____

_____

_____

Item: _____

Located:_____

Origin: _____

Meaning or Value:_____

Is there anyone special you would like to have this item   ☐ Yes   ☐ No

If so, whom:_____

What are your hopes regarding this item: _____

Why has this been special for you:_____

Other comments:

_____

_____

_____

PERSONAL PROPERTY ARCHIVE

Item: _____

Located:_____

Origin: _____

Meaning or Value:_____

Is there anyone special you would like to have this item   ☐ Yes   ☐ No

If so, whom:_____

What are your hopes regarding this item: _____

Why has this been special for you: _____

Other comments:

_____

_____

_____

Item: _____

Located:_____

Origin: _____

Meaning or Value:_____

Is there anyone special you would like to have this item   ☐ Yes   ☐ No

If so, whom:_____

What are your hopes regarding this item: _____

Why has this been special for you: _____

Other comments:

_____

_____

_____

PERSONAL PROPERTY ARCHIVE

Item: _____

Located:_____

Origin: _____

Meaning or Value:_____

Is there anyone special you would like to have this item   ☐ Yes   ☐ No

If so, whom:_____

What are your hopes regarding this item: _____

Why has this been special for you:_____

Other comments:

_____

_____

Item: _____

Located:_____

Origin: _____

Meaning or Value:_____

Is there anyone special you would like to have this item   ☐ Yes   ☐ No

If so, whom:_____

What are your hopes regarding this item: _____

Why has this been special for you:_____

Other comments:

_____

_____

If more Personal Property inventory space is needed, make a section for this in your separate notebook. More forms on www.sunrisesandsunsetsbook.com)

Loans and Outstanding Debts

In today's society, most of us have some type of existing loan or debt that we have secured to have something we need or want. This is an area to list such loans as a mortgage loan, car/auto loan, personal bank loan, student loan, money you may have borrowed and are paying back to someone (personal loans), a Rent-A-Center type of loan, a title loan, and even things you may have on lay-away and have paid into but still have a remaining balance until the items are yours free and clear.

In this area, use the forms to list any loans you have. And, over time, as the data becomes old, cross it out and date the time the loan was paid off in full so the record remains current to your existing life.

If you think nobody cares
if you're alive,
try missing a couple
of car payments.
~EARL WILSON

LOANS RECORD

Type of Loan:_____

Lender Name:_____

Address:_____

Phone:_____ Loan Number:_____

How is this loan paid:_____

How often is this loan paid:_____

Specifically, what was this loan for:_____

Date loan originated:_____

Date loan satisfied:_____

If this loan has been paid in full, Please mark this box with date satisfied and initial it.

☐ Date/Initials:_____

Type of Loan:_____

Lender Name:_____

Address:_____

Phone:_____ Loan Number:_____

How is this loan paid:_____

How often is this loan paid:_____

Specifically, what was this loan for:_____

Date loan originated:_____

Date loan satisfied:_____

If this loan has been paid in full, Please mark this box with date satisfied and initial it.

☐ Date/Initials:_____

Social Security information

Social Security is a program of elder age, unemployment, health, disability, and survivors' insurance maintained by the U.S. federal government through compulsory payments by specific employer and employee groups. It is also the theory or practice of providing economic security and social welfare for the individual through government programs maintained by moneys from public taxation.

Upon one's passing, there could be benefits available to eligible survivors. Since Social Security laws continually change, it is important to contact Social Security directly regarding specific questions. They can be reached at 1-800-772-1213 and also have local offices that can be accessed in person.

It is very important for your survivors to know that Social Security benefits are not paid automatically. One must apply for them. In this section, we will ensure you have your documents in order so that doing so will be trouble-free if something were to happen to you.

We discussed earlier in this book that the funeral home may assist with the filing of paperwork for your one-time lump sum death payment (LSDP), if applicable, to an eligible survivor, but definitely verify. However, for other potential survivors' benefits, paperwork will need to be submitted in a timely manner, and could include the need for the following documents: birth certificate of deceased, applicant's birth certificate, minor children's birth certificate(s), proof of disabled child over 18 years of age, funeral invoice, proof of previous year's income, dissolution of marriage proof, the deceased Social Security card or number, and perhaps other documents as requested.

For United States veterans, necessary documentation will include discharge papers (DD214); a certified copy of the death certificate; certificate of birth of the veteran's minor children, veteran's marriage certificate; and because regulations and stipulations change, it would be a good idea for survivors to contact the Department of Veteran's Affairs directly to ensure all benefits available are being accessed.

This will be a straightforward task for your survivors if and when the time arises for them to handle these matters, if you do as you have done with other sections of this book, and place the aforementioned documents, including a copy of your Social Security card, in your separate notebook and label the tab, "My Social Security Benefits."

SOCIAL SECURITY INFORMATION

My Social Security payment is received:_____

☐ Via automatic deposit into account number _____

at _____ bank on the _____ of each month.

OR

☐ Via checked mailed to me

    ☐ at my residence address

    ☐ at a Post Office Box

When you make a choice
you change the future.
~DEEPAK CHOPRA

Medicare/Tri-Care/Medicaid/Railroad Benefits/Other

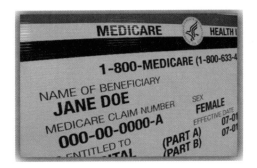

Medicare is a federally funded health care and hospital insurance program for people age 65 and older and some disabled people. Medicare was enacted in 1965, as one of the Great Society programs of President Lyndon B. Johnson. However, it was first proposed as a medical care program for the elderly during the 1940's by President Harry S. Truman. In any event, Medicare has become a household name for those turning 65.

Tricare is a health care program of the United States Department of Defense Military Health System. Tricare provides civilian health benefits for military personnel, military retirees, and their dependents, including some members of the reserves.

Medicaid is for people, regardless of age, whose income is below the threshold to pay for healthcare. While administered on a state level, matching funds are provided from the federal government. Medicaid services and options vary from state to state.

During my decade and a half of owning an insurance firm, only once did I have the unique pleasure of working with a gentleman with Railroad Medicare so I would estimate it is rather infrequent, so I found it quite an honor! I always enjoyed the challenge of learning new facets of my profession.

Railroad Medicare is for people who have worked more than ten years for the railroad and are receiving benefits from the Railroad Retirement Board. However, services, benefits, eligibility, claims and enrollment are provided through Railroad Medicare, otherwise currently known as Palmetto GBA Medicare which administers Medicare health insurance for the Centers of Medicare and Medicaid.

MEDICARE/TRI-CARE/RAILROAD/MEDICAID/ OTHER INFORMATION

Do you have Medicare/Tri-Care/Railroad/Medicaid Benefits?

☐ Yes   ☐ No

If yes, describe what benefits you have:

_____

_____

What is your Benefits Claim Number (off of your card):

_____

If Medicare, Please fill in your Medicare Part A and Part B effective date:

_____

If other coverage, please fill in pertinent dates or other information below:

_____

_____

If you are on Medicare, do you have a Medicare Supplement or Medicare Advantage type plan in addition to your Medicare:

☐ Yes   ☐ No

If yes, please describe: (in the "My Insurance Information" section of this book, you will list specifics)

_____

_____

List any other relevant details related to your coverage below:

_____

_____

_____

Pensions and /or Retirement Funds

(check which applies)

☐ I do receive a pension or retirement check.

☐ I do **NOT** receive a pension or retirement check.

If you do receive a pension or retirement check, please complete the following:

These funds arrive _____ monthly or:_____

The funds are received by: ☐ direct deposit   ☐ monthly check by mail

These funds are deposited into (bank name):_____

in the amount of $_____

Details:

_____

_____

_____

_____

These funds arrive _____ monthly or:_____

The funds are received by: ☐ direct deposit   ☐ monthly check by mail

These funds are deposited into (bank name):_____

in the amount of $_____

Details:

_____

_____

_____

_____

Other Services Utilized

 In our everyday lives, we access a lot of modern conveniences that were once not considered a customary way of living. Not everyone mows his or her own lawn, and some people have traded in the push mower for the luxury of yard service. Some people are not interested in the everyday maintenance required for many of the amenities we enjoy in life. Swimming pools can be maintained by a pool service, and pest control companies keep out the uninvited guests from our dwellings.

There are also the overlooked recreational pleasures and even business expenses such as internet and cable subscriptions or even annual theatre memberships. Try to consider all of the items you access in your everyday life and list them in this section. You may want to look at your checking account to be sure you are not overlooking anything that is automatically paid for via electronic funds transfer each month.

The Kaleidoscope of colour

which is my life,

shows the interesting choices

I've made along the way.

~ANTIE KOEKIE

SERVICES UTILIZED LOG

Service:_____

Company:_____

Person of contact:_____

Address/Phone:_____

How is this paid for:_____

Frequency of payment:_____

Is this a contract or month to month:_____

Service:_____

Company:_____

Person of contact:_____

Address/Phone:_____

How is this paid for:_____

Frequency of payment:_____

Is this a contract or month to month:_____

Service:_____

Company:_____

Person of contact:_____

Address/Phone:_____

How is this paid for:_____

Frequency of payment:_____

Is this a contract or month to month:_____

Outstanding Personal, Business or Legal Matters

At any given time in our lives, we seem to be in the midst of unfinished business. If you have ongoing matters yet unsettled, this section is the place to list them and provide some information as to any details surrounding these affairs. This is to include personal unfinished business, business matters, and legal issues.

Perhaps you have unresolved litigation, lawsuits, or even a business in the midst of a sale but not yet complete. Any unfinished business of any kind can be listed in the space below. This is a very ambiguous category, so the more information you can provide the better. Obviously, as these issues get resolved throughout your life, you will cross off the former material or remove it to keep the details current.

Old friends pass away,

new friends appear.

It is just like the days.

An old day passes, a new day arrives.

The important thing

is to make it meaningful:

a meaningful friend –

or a meaningful day.

~DALAI LAMA

IMPORTANT BUSINESS / PERSONAL MATTERS

Type of Matter (check which applies):

         ☐ personal   ☐ business   ☐ legal   ☐ other

Describe:_____

What is left unfinished regarding this matter?

_____

What other parties are involved in this situation?

_____

Who is the point of contact to attempt to resolve this matter?

Name: _____

Address:_____ Phone:_____

Any additional details: _____

Type of Matter (check which applies):

         ☐ personal   ☐ business   ☐ legal   ☐ other

Describe:_____

What is left unfinished regarding this matter?

_____

What other parties are involved in this situation?

_____

Who is the point of contact to attempt to resolve this matter?

Name: _____

Address:_____ Phone:_____

Any additional details: _____

IMPORTANT BUSINESS / PERSONAL MATTERS

Type of Matter (check which applies):

☐ personal   ☐ business   ☐ legal   ☐ other

Describe:_____

What is left unfinished regarding this matter?

_____

What other parties are involved in this situation?

Who is the point of contact to attempt to resolve this matter?

Name: _____

Address:_____ Phone:_____

Any additional details: _____

Type of Matter (check which applies):

☐ personal   ☐ business   ☐ legal   ☐ other

Describe:_____

What is left unfinished regarding this matter?

What other parties are involved in this situation?

Who is the point of contact to attempt to resolve this matter?

Name: _____

Address:_____ Phone:_____

Any additional details: _____

Anything and Everything Else!

I wish I could cover everything for everyone in a little over 200 pages, but that would be impossible. So, this section is a "wild card" of sorts. This is where you will capture anything else pertaining to you that hasn't been covered in the previous sections outlined related to your personal and business matters. Use this section to place those details; and if there is sensitive related information, you know by now where to put that and how to organize it accordingly.

_____

_____

_____

_____

_____

_____

_____

_____

_____

_____

_____

_____

_____

_____

_____

_____

_____

_____

_____

_____

_____

_____

_____

SECTION 3

NOTHING LEFT UNSAID—
LOVE, LIVE, CELEBRATE!

CHAPTER 14

YOUR Life! YOUR Legacy!

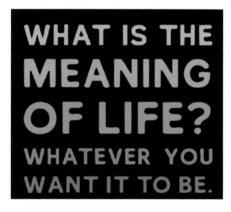

Today is yours! But, when your Final Sunset occurs, from that moment on will be your legacy. Your legacy is all that is left behind. Notice I did not say the word "things" you leave behind, or even "people" you leave behind. When I speak of your legacy, I mean even beyond possessions and heritage. I mean your legacy in terms of how your life can be regarded as significant and cherished beyond your state of living and provide encouragement and inspiration to those who continue to exist in your absence. The message that continues to live in your immortality is the intangible legacy you leave behind and the one I am asking you to consider most throughout this section.

Times are constantly changing. Many people believe that the good ol' days were the best days. However, we may find that countering that belief is the younger generation who may claim that the modern era is simply the best. But the journey from old-fashioned to modern-era encompasses much more than just progressing technology and more immediate access to contemporary amenities. It also introduces a cultural transformation affecting important character traits and outlooks on life, such as values, standards, and principles.

Study after study substantiates that the elders of a culture offer undeniable knowledge and perceptive guidance to younger generations. When this information is passed down through the generations, the progeny acquires a keen advantage in life skills and gains a fostered aptitude for both executing those life principles as well as passing down those same standards, morals, and ideals to their offspring as well.

This tradition has been carried out since the dawn of time. However, society is shifting to less family time and more societal demands. In the process, many families are not able to uphold the traditions of information exchange that once defined families and their historical genealogical fingerprint.

> I do nothing but go about persuading you all,
> old and young alike, not to take thought for your persons
> or your properties, but chiefly to care about
> the greatest improvement of the soul.
> I tell you that virtue is not given by money,
> but that from virtue comes money
> and every other good of man, public as well as private.
> This is my teaching, and if this is the doctrine
> which corrupts the youth,
> I am a mischievous person.
> ~SOCRATES

Drive-thru dining and fast-food convenience has become a staple replacement to what once was the ever-important family dinner. But the family dinner was more than a meal. It was a time for bonding, friendship, and camaraderie. It was a time to solidify the ties that bind. It was a time to hash out arguments and to resolve them. It was a time to establish direction, forge plans, and gain support. It was also a time to share our successes, grudges, disappointments, and news in a safe haven of others required to listen as long as food was still on the table.

In some families, due to stressful financial demands, the infrastructure of the family dinner has vanished into the abyss of bills and debt. Many families require both heads of households to work just to survive. In other families, a single parent struggles to do alone what it normally would take two. And, there are also grandparents raising grandchildren as they are facing challenges of their own. The demands of the ever-changing world are far and wide.

While holidays still offer a wonderful way for families to still connect, they are so full of hustle and bustle, there seems to be little time for relaxing moments of sharing. So, while there is fun and enjoyment, the activities and festivities do not often lend themselves to one-on-one time or moments of deeper reflection.

I recently officiated a funeral, and a family member whom I had not seen in over a decade came up to me and said, "Our family doesn't have family reunions; that's what weddings and funerals are for." Well, the truth was, there was a lot of genuineness to her comment as dismal as it was. And, in that sobering moment we all vowed to do a better job about connecting with one another because we truly enjoyed getting together. We just rarely moved enough stuff out of our daily lives to make the plans to do so.

There is love in our hearts no matter how long it's been since we've seen each other. They are part of my legacy and part of me. I don't want to let it slip away. And, your legacy could get lost if you don't share it here, as well as in person. That is why it is so important that we take the time to connect, embrace, slow down, and cherish.

In the next chapter, take the time and enjoy yourself as you share all about YOU!

> We must be willing to let go
> of the life we have planned,
> so as to have the life
> that is waiting for us.
> ~E.M. FORSTER

CHAPTER 15

Me, Myself, and I!

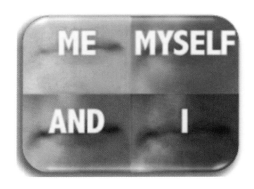

In this section, I am asking you not only to share information about yourself, but also family traditions, practices, and beliefs that make your family distinctive, special, and out of the ordinary. Perhaps there are customs or special traditions in your family that you have always incorporated or carried out, and you wish to ensure they continue on in your family in your absence. Without you, this information may never be passed down again. So take your time and share as much as you wish in these next few pages.

Some of the information I am asking you to archive will be personal thoughts and responses. Others will be facts as they relate to your life. Feel free to complete the sections that speak to you and that you feel you have something of relevance to share. And, most of all, don't rush. This area of the book is one to be enjoyed both by you as you formulate your responses and by the readers of your entries at a later time. Visualize your readers flipping through the pages of this book as they immerse themselves in thoughts of you and learn ALL ABOUT YOU!

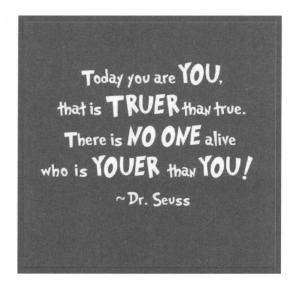

Today you are YOU,
that is TRUER than true.
There is NO ONE alive
who is YOUER than YOU!

~ Dr. Seuss

ALL ABOUT: _____

SPECIAL DATES AND ANNIVERSARIES IN MY LIFE:

Date: _____ Occasion: _____

Date: _____ Occasion: _____

Date: _____ Occasion: _____

Date: _____ Occasion: _____

Date: _____ Occasion: _____

Date: _____ Occasion: _____

Date: _____ Occasion: _____

Date: _____ Occasion: _____

Any additional notes or information relating to dates or occasions?

_____

_____

_____

_____

_____

_____

_____

_____

_____

_____

_____

_____

_____

_____

_____

_____

FAMILY TRADITIONS

Are there any family traditions that you cherish or would like to continue being honored occasions in your family? If so, please list and describe them below.

_____

_____

_____

_____

_____

_____

_____

_____

_____

_____

_____

_____

_____

_____

_____

_____

_____

_____

_____

_____

_____

_____

_____

_____

Experience is the name
everyone gives to mistakes.
~OSCAR WILDE

Are there any secrets in your life that have been unrevealed that you would like to disclose? If yes, please respond below.

Remember to make decisions cautiously as to who will read this information and how this may be taken when you are no longer here to provide additional supporting details. Personal information intended for specific people can be shared in your "Letters to Loved Ones section," if you prefer.

_____

_____

_____

_____

_____

_____

_____

_____

_____

_____

_____

_____

_____

_____

_____

_____

_____

_____

_____

_____

An investment in knowledge
pays the best interest.
~BENJAMIN FRANKLIN

What are your thoughts regarding the afterlife or what happens when we die?

_____

_____

_____

_____

_____

_____

_____

_____

_____

If you believe in the afterlife, who do you hope is waiting on the other side to greet you?

_____

_____

_____

_____

_____

_____

_____

_____

_____

We complain because rose
bushes have thorns,
or rejoice because thorn
bushes have roses.
~ABRAHAM LINCOLN

Has there been anyone you have not made peace with or any apologies that you wish to address in writing? If yes, please explain and describe below.

It is important to make it clear as to who this information is regarding and /or intended for and be sure it is acceptable for multiple viewers. Also remember that personal and private entries can be saved for your "Letters to Loved Ones" section.

_____
_____
_____
_____
_____
_____
_____
_____
_____
_____

If you could use three words or phrases to describe your life philosophy what would they be?

1. _____
2. _____
3. _____

What are some things most people may not know about you?

_____
_____
_____
_____
_____
_____
_____
_____
_____

What mistakes have you made and what have you learned?

_____
_____
_____
_____
_____
_____
_____
_____

What is your earliest memory?

_____
_____
_____
_____
_____
_____
_____
_____

What are your favorite memories?

_____
_____
_____
_____
_____
_____
_____
_____

What is one of the proudest moments in your life?

_____
_____
_____
_____
_____
_____
_____
_____

What are the things that have changed the most in your life?

_____
_____
_____
_____
_____
_____
_____
_____

What do you know now that you didn't know when you were younger?

_____
_____
_____
_____
_____
_____
_____
_____

Looking back, what held you back the most in your life?

_____
_____
_____
_____
_____
_____
_____
_____
_____

Looking back, what was your biggest personal asset in life?

_____
_____
_____
_____
_____
_____
_____
_____
_____

Looking back on life, what do you wish you had done?

_____
_____
_____
_____
_____
_____
_____
_____
_____

Some of the biggest events in your life included:

_____

_____

_____

_____

_____

_____

_____

_____

Some of the saddest moments in your life have been:

_____

_____

_____

_____

_____

_____

_____

_____

_____

Some of the happiest times in your life included:

_____

_____

_____

_____

_____

_____

_____

_____

_____

Your biggest fears have been:

_____

_____

_____

_____

_____

_____

_____

What has mattered to you most in life?

_____

_____

_____

_____

_____

_____

_____

_____

If you could change anything about the world what would it be?

_____

_____

_____

_____

If you could have one wish, what would it be?

_____

_____

_____

_____

_____

Two more wishes?

_____

_____

_____

_____

Who was the most influential person in your life and why?

_____

_____

_____

_____

What are your favorite books?

_____

_____

_____

_____

What technologies, machines, or inventions were new when you were a child and how did they impact your life?

_____

_____

_____

_____

What significant events occurred when you were a child?

_____

_____

_____

_____

_____

_____

What type of clothes were popular when you were a child?

_____
_____
_____
_____
_____

What are your favorite movies?

_____
_____
_____
_____

Who is your favorite famous person in history? Why?

_____
_____
_____
_____
_____
_____

Who is your favorite movie star?

_____
_____
_____
_____

What pet(s) have you loved the most in your life?

_____
_____
_____
_____

What was the most difficult lesson you ever learned?

_____

_____

_____

_____

What family value(s) have helped you the most in life and how?

_____

_____

_____

_____

Which family members have helped you the most in life and how?

_____

_____

_____

_____

If you could have a "do over," what would you do over and how would your life be different?

_____

_____

_____

_____

_____

_____

_____

_____

_____

_____

_____

_____

What do you want to be remembered for?

_____
_____
_____
_____
_____
_____
_____
_____
_____
_____

What do you believe the meaning of life may be?

_____
_____
_____
_____
_____
_____
_____
_____
_____
_____
_____

Be kind whenever possible.
It is always possible.
~DALAI LAMA

What does your life philosophy include?

_____

_____

_____

_____

_____

Some things you may be leaving unfulfilled or wish you had done but never did include:

_____

_____

_____

_____

_____

What is the best advice you can offer?

_____

_____

_____

_____

_____

_____

_____

_____

_____

_____

_____

_____

_____

_____

_____

_____

Some things you would like others to know but have not been able to say are:

_____
_____
_____
_____
_____

You were always the happiest when:

_____
_____
_____
_____
_____

Your parting words of wisdom or love are:

_____
_____
_____
_____
_____
_____
_____
_____
_____
_____
_____

The greater part of our happiness
depends on our dispositions,
and not our circumstances.
~MARTHA WASHINGTON

Private and Personal Extras:

(Here, add anything not captured in the previous sections that you wish to include.)

_____

_____

_____

_____

_____

_____

_____

_____

_____

_____

_____

Keep your thoughts positive
because your thoughts become your words.
Keep your words positive
because your words become your behavior.
Keep your behavior positive
because your behavior becomes your habits.
Keep your habits positive
because your habits become your values.
Keep your values positive
because your values become your destiny.
~MAHATMA GANDHI

CHAPTER 16
Important Family Health History

In this area, please list any chronic illnesses or family history of disease or ailments that you feel may be valuable information for your family to know.

You can also write the individual or relationship to you, and please include cause of death where applicable or known. This type of information is often highly valuable medical knowledge that is often lost in families when not passed down or shared.

In situations of adoptions, if you are privy to family information of the adoptive family, enter it here as well. Any details known may prove valuable at a later date. If no known information exists, leave blank.

It's not how old you are;

it's how you are old.

~JULES RENARD

IMPORTANT FAMILY HEALTH HISTORY

Name: _____

Relationship to you:_____

Health ailments, diseases, chronic illnesses or medical conditions

_____

Date of birth and death (if still living, write "Living"):_____

Cause of death (if applicable):_____

_____

Name: _____

Relationship to you:_____

Health ailments, diseases, chronic illnesses or medical conditions

_____

Date of birth and death (if still living, write "Living"):_____

Cause of death (if applicable):_____

_____

Name: _____

Relationship to you:_____

Health ailments, diseases, chronic illnesses or medical conditions

_____

Date of birth and death (if still living, write "Living"):_____

Cause of death (if applicable):_____

_____

IMPORTANT FAMILY HEALTH HISTORY

Name: _____

Relationship to you:_____

Health ailments, diseases, chronic illnesses or medical conditions

_____

Date of birth and death (if still living, write "Living"):_____

Cause of death (if applicable):_____

Name: _____

Relationship to you:_____

Health ailments, diseases, chronic illnesses or medical conditions

_____

Date of birth and death (if still living, write "Living"):_____

Cause of death (if applicable):_____

Name: _____

Relationship to you:_____

Health ailments, diseases, chronic illnesses or medical conditions

_____

Date of birth and death (if still living, write "Living"):_____

Cause of death (if applicable):_____

CHAPTER 17

Family Tree and Family History

MY FAMILY TREE

If your family tree has its share of intriguing people, colorful characters, flamboyant folks, a random black sheep, and even an interesting nut or two—well, that probably makes your family pretty normal! And, it makes family reunions, gatherings, and celebrations quite exciting and entertaining! Regardless of who is nesting in your family tree, family is, as they say....FAMILY.

F=Familiar, A=Ambivalent, M=Matrix, I=Intricate, L=Love, Y=You; this is how I define FAMILY; Familiar Ambivalent Matrix of Intricate Love for YOU! If your family is a bit different you can switch the word matrix out for madness and intricate for insane. You can customize my acronym to fit your family dynamic.

Insanity runs in my family.

It practically gallops.

~Cary Grant

You may already have a family tree; and if that is the case, good for you! But, if you don't it is a lot of fun to put one together and a wonderful history for your family to enjoy for years to come. In my family, a lot of our history was preserved in the mind of my great aunt, who died nearly a decade ago at the age of 96. She knew our history quite well. Unfortunately, when she told the rest of us in our younger years, well...the truth is, we probably weren't putting our listening ears on very well. For some reason, it seems that "stuff" only gets really interesting as we grow older. And, I guess "I'm older," because now it seems like a pretty interesting topic for discussion.

So do your family a favor and don't rely on their interest level. Put it in writing. The next project I will ask you to complete is your family tree. The family tree included is a simple one for four generations. If you feel the desire to dig into deeper family roots, feel free. If you have access to a computer or have the program EXCEL, you will have a variety of templates you can access. Additionally, for those of you more ambitious and with greater curiosity, there are many online sites in which you can delve into your past ancestry with ease if you so desire.

Your family tree is a very important part of your family's history and lineage, and future generations will greatly appreciate the time you take to ensure details of the family are not lost with each passing generation.

NOTE: When filling out your family tree, put in not only the names but the years of births and deaths if you can.

Before most people start boasting
about their family tree,
they usually do a good pruning job.
~O.A. BATTISTA

Now that you have completed the family tree diagram, you can write in some details about specific family members, mentioned or not, and some family associations that you believe may exist but may have not even necessarily been determined or validated. In my particular case, I had been privy to legends of a family association with an infamous frontiersman during the American Revolution in the 1700's that is said to be related and was a bit of an outlaw and rebel. I look forward to looking this up one day to validate it and find out what made him so notorious. So, outlaws and in-laws and everything in between, this kind of information would be an exciting and interesting bread trail to leave your family if it is yet to be confirmed.

Some families have a history that includes famous people, and you may wish to reference this association. You may also delve further back into your family's history and share any particular members that will not make the 4-generation list herein but may be noteworthy!

Have fun with this! Your family will treasure your work and you will enjoy it too!

"When your mother asks,
"Do you want a piece of advice?"
it's a mere formality.
It doesn't matter if you answer yes or no.
You're going to get it anyway."
~ERMA BOMBECK

NOTABLE FAMILY MEMBERS

Name: _____

Family relationship:_____

Era lived or dates of birth and death (if know):_____

Known for:_____

Other details about this individual:

_____

_____

_____

Name: _____

Family relationship:_____

Era lived or dates of birth and death (if know):_____

Known for:_____

Other details about this individual:

_____

_____

_____

Name: _____

Family relationship:_____

Era lived or dates of birth and death (if know):_____

Known for:_____

Other details about this individual:

_____

_____

_____

NOTABLE FAMILY MEMBERS

Name: _____

Family relationship:_____

Era lived or dates of birth and death (if know):_____

Known for:_____

Other details about this individual:

_____

_____

_____

Name: _____

Family relationship:_____

Era lived or dates of birth and death (if know):_____

Known for:_____

Other details about this individual:

_____

_____

_____

Name: _____

Family relationship:_____

Era lived or dates of birth and death (if know):_____

Known for:_____

Other details about this individual:

_____

_____

_____

List any pertinent family details such as descent, migration, immigration, etc., in the space provided below.

_____

_____

_____

_____

_____

_____

_____

_____

_____

_____

_____

_____

_____

_____

_____

_____

_____

_____

_____

_____

_____

_____

_____

Do not dwell of the past,

do not dream of the future,

concentrate the mind on the present moment.

~BUDDHA

CHAPTER 18

Dear Loved One

To live and love is a beautiful thing! But leaving those we love is not such a jubilant thought. We have certainly discussed in this book the notion that we have no ability to predict when we will actually engage in our farewell. For each person, it is the great unknown mystery. Some deaths are sudden and unexpected. Some are impending and agonizing and known in advance, despite the wish otherwise. And some deaths are even welcomed following a taxing and debilitating journey of disease and ailment and seen as a means to end the pain and suffering of a loved one. We just don't know when we will part ways with our familiar existence known as life.

> Guilt is perhaps the
> Most painful companion of death.
> ~ELISABETH KüBLER-ROSS

In this section, *Dear Loved One*, you will be able to take your time and write a meaningful and personal letter to those you love so very much. Because each and every relationship we have is unique and personal and built on its own set of experiences, memories, and meaning, these letters will each be exclusive to their intended recipient. There is so much that can be said to those you love and cherish. These letters can continue and grow over time as life unfolds more exciting moments and you consider new things you wish to convey.

We often worry about passing unexpectedly and wonder if those we leave behind will remember or know how we really feel. These letters can help lessen your anxiety in that respect as they will give you a sense of comfort because you have left your thoughts and feelings for them in the event of unforeseen circumstances. So feel free to add to these letters or begin new ones over your life course. The separate notebook you have created and are using for your other important documents you are creating from this book will be the perfect place to allow you to neatly store these letters until the time they may be read by the ones you love. This is a very enriching and therapeutic exercise and one you will feel wonderful about doing!

So, who are you writing to? Make a list below and begin your first step of getting started.

I WILL WRITE *DEAR LOVED ONE* LETTERS TO THE FOLLOWING PEOPLE:

_____

_____

_____

_____

_____

_____

_____

_____

_____

_____

_____

_____

_____

_____

_____

_____

_____

_____

_____

_____

_____

Your *Dear Loved One* letters should be highly personal in nature. Consider the following questions and thoughts when writing yours to those you love.

What do they mean to you?

What role do they play in your life?

What, if anything, do you want to ask their forgiveness for?

What message do you want them to carry with them?

What do you hope YOU were to them?

What are your hopes for their future?

How will you ask them to deal with their grief from your passing?

Do you need to forgive them for something?

What permissions do you wish to leave them?

What aspirations do you want for them (to continue) to achieve?

What insight do you have for them?

What are your happiest memories with them?

What do you ask of them?

What should they NEVER forget?

When the going gets rough....?

What do you think of them? What do you admire?

How do THEY help YOU with life? What inspiration do they offer you?

What character trait do you admire about them?

What should they make sure they never lose?

Advice on living from here on....

Lovingly clear up a misunderstanding to offer peace to them moving forward...

Anything else you wish to convey.

I will use this platform to address another area that may become a part of your *Dear Loved One* letter writing, in hopes that it may help some people who unknowingly may find themselves in such a circumstance.

If you want a love message to be heard,

it has got to be sent out.

To keep a lamp burning,

we have to keep putting oil in it.

~MOTHER TERESA

As an insurance broker, I worked with many people who were planning their insurance affairs. In doing so, their insurance allocations regarding beneficiary percentages were made known to me. They often shared with me why they were doing what they were doing, not so much to justify, but to determine their best approach in regard to their life-insurance planning. My capacity was one of which I was dutifully entrusted with their confidentiality, and this was a professional ethic I took quite seriously. The truth was, I usually understood their reasoning and it actually made sense. But, I often wondered if they ever told their kids. Many times I posed this question to my clients, and they usually responded with, "They'll find out soon enough."

I found myself a bit encumbered with this dynamic, knowing that when this lovely person passed away, there would be so much anguish and sadness for their loss. Then, there would be the life insurance distribution. Then, there would be the news that one child received 25% and the other child received 75%. Then, there would be discord between siblings—hurt feelings, dismay, and even anger perhaps with the child that had received the larger percentage or guilt about receiving more. I always felt a little anguish over the fact that there was a reasonable and viable explanation behind their logic but knowing that their child may not be privy to the information herself—something I really felt was needed and deserved.

Death is final. There is no more time for questions. Hence, there is no more time for answers. After someone you love dies, the "why?" word is a tough one to go unanswered. It is akin to an erosion or an ulcer in some instances, simply because the answers die with the individual and the "mystery and

193

maybe's" can often lead to more "whys." If there is something you have done, or are going to do that may be misperceived, misunderstood or otherwise—and I mean anything, obviously not just insurance as in the previous example—you may want to consider giving that special person the gift of explanation, details, and reasoning. This way, they can understand and accept your decisions and not harbor resentment unnecessarily when you are no longer here to resolve the matter. You cannot imagine how much burden could be lifted by addressing these matters and allowing them to reflect on your memory with love and be able to live their lives free of resentment and anguish with a peaceful soul.

So, I am sharing situations like these here, in this section, for you to consider. My example is insurance for the sake of dialogue. But there are so many areas of life where similar situations of misunderstandings can be misconstrued. When writing this book and writing in general, a tactic I use is to write furiously for days on end. It is almost like cramming for an exam. Then, I walk away for several days. But, I am only away from it physically. While I am away, while I am doing all of my other things, I am thinking of the words, each sentence, the pages, and its content. The reels are playing in my head. In my mind, the edits are being done. I call this process, "mentally marinating." This is one of the most important components of my writing and where some of my best ideas and reworks are spawned. So, I guess I am asking you to "mentally marinate" about anything in your life that, in laymen's terms, "may need some explaining." You can only do it now. Later may never come.

There may be things in life you do, things that appear unfair, unreasonable, insane, unjustifiable, un-"something"—but you have YOUR reasons—or at least you have an explanation. Maybe you don't have an explanation but someone needs an acknowledgement that you know it may have been unjust or unfair and you are sorry. Sometimes people care little about the actual action and more about the fact that it can simply be acknowledged so they can feel respected and honored.

In my specific gentleman's case, he knew his daughter would be burdened with his credit card debt for which he wanted her extra share of the life insurance money to help pay. She also had been helping him out financially and he wanted to repay her some of that money. Additionally, her children, his grandchildren were hoping to go to college, and he was hoping to contribute a small portion to bringing that dream to a reality.

The most beautiful people we have ever Known
are those who have Known defeat,
Known suffering, Known struggle, Known loss,
and have pulled themselves out of the depths.
These people have an appreciation,
a sensitivity, and an understanding of life
that fills them with compassion, gentleness,
and a deep loving concern.
Beautiful people do not just happen.
~ELISABETH KüBLER-ROSS

Explore your life and be sure you are not leaving any potential mystery burdens such as these that may cause anguish and confusion for your loved ones. Your *Dear Loved One* letters are meant to send a telegram of love from the other side if you will. Search your soul far and wide to think about anything you may want to say and use this opportunity to share your words and convey your thoughts and feelings, even if that means clarifying anything or explaining things.

Remember to store your *Dear Loved One* letters in the special place you are housing your other important documents. You may even "date" these special letters to be read on special occasions.

Unfortunately, some of us may pass before "our time." In such instances, one very special thing that we can do to still "show" for important events we fear we will miss is to write letters to our loved ones to be opened on those most joyous celebrations. For someone who may be surrendering to accepting their own departure, I cannot help but imagine the comfort and healing one might encounter when writing these letters. These letters serve the writer as much as the recipient and are highly therapeutic and emotionally cleansing.

I'LL BE HERE
By Holley Kelley

Did you know I loved you before you were born?

I thought I heard Angels trumpeting their horns.

My love for you soars to Heavenly heights.

Look up; you'll see me in the stars shining bright.

I'll be here like the matter and energy of earth.

I'll be here every day from your moment of birth.

I am in you and you are of me.

My love for you is everlasting.

Unfortunately, we each know of young lives taken too soon by terminal illnesses or other misfortunes. This is a great project for people facing or concerned about these circumstances. While it will bring tears, it will also provide joy and comfort. So, consider these ideas as they relate to your life. "To _____, on your wedding day," "To _____, on your 18th Birthday," and so forth. The words you write in these letters will both keep you present, and serve as a present in the hearts and spirit of those who read them.

This is a great way for you to change the future for those who will be missing you and allow your true essence to continue to be part of special occasions of your loved ones in the future. Take your time with these letters. Write as many as you want. Think of everything you may be concerned about missing and address them one by one. More importantly, be inspired to open up thoughts, feelings, and emotions and pour onto paper YOUR UNDENIABLE LOVE!

TOGETHER, FOREVER
By Holley Kelley

I wrote you a letter and put it away.

The words I wrote are things I can't say.

They are thoughts I feel and emotions so pure.

The truths they contain will surely endure.

One day, you will read the words I composed.

And you will feel my presence purely exposed.

I will echo through the pages, and into your heart,

In that moment it will be, as if we're not apart.

My letters to you are part of me you can treasure —

It's a way we can be close; together, forever.

CHAPTER 19
Checklists

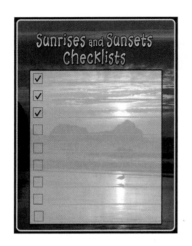

No workbook would be complete without a checklist! And if you are anything like me while writing this book, you did not accomplish things in order. You may have been all over the place. For that reason, I have included a checklist for you to check off items as you complete them. Please reference this sheet as a reminder of what you still need to do to complete your final planning.

Once you have all the boxes checked off, you can breathe easy! You have done it! You deserve way more than a gold star! But you do get the peace of mind as a bonus for a challenging task accomplished and behind you! Hats off to you! And, please accept my congratulations!

The best time to plant a tree
is 20 years ago.
The second best time is now.
~CHINESE PROVERB

Sunrises and Sunsets
FINAL PLANNING CHECKLIST

☐ Read this book!

☐ Tell your family you are working on this book and urge your friends to get one and plan their final affairs as well!

☐ Create a separate notebook to keep important items compiled from this book organized! Maintain in a safe, private location.

☐ Create Your Bucket List!

☐ Create your "KICK"-the-Bucket List!

☐ Complete Your Advance Directives

☐ Complete your Last Will and Testament

☐ Write Your Own Obituary

☐ Plan Your Burial or Cremation details

☐ Plan your funeral or memorial

☐ Personal Accounts logged

☐ Safety Deposit boxes logged

☐ Finances Logged

☐ Insurance Logged

☐ Credit/Debit Card information logged

☐ Personal Property Archive logged

☐ Loans and Outstanding Debts logged

☐ Social Security logged

☐ Medicare/Tricare/Railroad benefits logged

☐ Pensions, Retirement and Other Income logged

☐ Other Services I Utilize logged

☐ Outstanding Personal Matters logged

☐ Outstanding Personal/Business or Legal Matters logged

☐ Workbook "All About Me" Pages complete

☐ Family Health Archive completed

☐ Family Tree completed

☐ Additional Family History completed

☐ All Dear Loved One Letters written:

To_____

To_____

To_____

To_____

To_____

To_____

To_____

To_____

To_____

☐ I Completed THIS checklist!

If task directly above is completed, CELEBRATE!!!

Additional Planning Objectives or Personal Items Not Covered in this book:

_____
_____
_____
_____
_____
_____
_____
_____
_____
_____
_____
_____
_____
_____
_____
_____
_____
_____
_____
_____
_____
_____
_____
_____
_____
_____
_____

The following checklist is what I am calling a "Survivor's Checklist." In the event of your passing, this list should assist in expediting important matters relating to your affairs. Please let your designated family members know that this book and the Survivor Checklist exist so they may benefit from its use.

Obviously, this is not a list requiring anything of you. We have created and prepared this book for the benefit of both for you and those you love. With that said, this list is a small compass for them when they will need some direction. While there may be additional things for them to handle, this will certainly get them headed in the right direction and shepherd them, initially, through an essential process.

It's only when we truly know and
understand that we have a limited time on earth—
and that we have no way of knowing
when our time is up—
that we will begin to live each day to the fullest,
as if it was the only one we had.
~ELISABETH KüBLER-ROSS

SURVIVOR'S CHECKLIST

NOTE TO SURVIVORS: The basic details to most of these items are more than likely located within this book and the separate notebook maintained.

☐ If applicable, secure financial instruments of deceased immediately, such as cash, checks, credit cards, and valuables. Secure home/dwelling access.

☐ Contact people on Contact List in this book including professional contacts such as funeral home, lawyer, accountant, insurance broker, etc.

☐ Meet with funeral home, lawyer, accountant, insurance broker, financial planner, if necessary, for related business matters. **Note: you may need to obtain multiple copies of the death certificates**, will, trust, tax returns, etc. before you meet with certain professionals.

☐ Contact Social Security at 1-800-772-1213 to apply for appropriate benefits or visit a local Social Security branch.

☐ Apply for veterans benefits, if applicable.

☐ Notify banks. Find out what steps are required to move forward with accounts. Inquire how to cancel direct deposits, if applicable.

☐ Notify credit card companies and cancel credit cards. Obtain necessary information for closing and settling accounts.

☐ Notify mortgage company or other outstanding personal loans.

☐ Notify department of motor vehicles, if applicable.

☐ Contact post office and/or access post office box to handle mail, etc.

☐ Submit appropriate forms to IRS, such as tax returns, etc. Consult with a professional tax consultant, attorney or estate lawyer for assistance in completing and submitting these forms.

☐ Handle any real estate property transfers, collect rent, etc.

☐ Notify other appropriate entities or organizations as deemed applicable.

☐ Arrange to collect personal items from place of work, if applicable.

☐ Review this book to ensure nothing is left uncovered. This will definitely help ensure all personal and business matters are handled.

☐ Make a list of additional items beyond this that should be done below:

_____

_____

_____

_____

_____

_____

_____

_____

_____

_____

_____

_____

_____

_____

_____

_____

_____

_____

_____

_____

_____

_____

CHAPTER 20

Deputized Death Wrangler!

As you have probably garnered by now, I have been a life-long horse enthusiast. I often tell people I am a girl born in the wrong century. I am fascinated with the old west and Native American cultures of days gone by. I like to keep things simple. While life back then may not have been easy, I do believe it was much simpler than things are today. And, yet we have many wonderful benefits of a modern society of which we all can count our blessings! When writing this book I really attempted to identify what exactly it was I wanted to do with "death."

It isn't death that's complicated. There's living and there's dying. That is a simple and straightforward concept. It's how we, as a society and as individuals, deal with death—or fail to deal with death—that has been the challenge. I knew if I was going to write about this subject and attempt to help people, I needed to identify my mission and set my literary compass to navigate accordingly.

I decided that I wanted to make death less scary and frightening. I wanted to make the subject easy and inspirational. I wanted to encourage people to get their final affairs in order and advance-care planning done. I wanted to help people to connect and share vital and benevolent details with their loved ones. And, somehow, horses end up in a lot of what I do and it happened here too.

So, in considering how I wanted to tackle death in this book, I decided I wanted to be a "death wrangler" of sorts.

In my first interview about this book I was asked what I wanted to do with death and I shared this concept with the writer, Alison Reeger-Cook. Interestingly enough, the first article ever published about this book was titled, "Death Wrangler." The label, as often occurs, tended to stick. Thereby, keeping with that, in completing this book, you too have wrangled death in your own way!

Therefore, I proudly and officially declare you a "Deputy Death Wrangler!"

While we're just having fun, what you have done isn't trivial at all. You have completed the many important matters, projects, and exercises in this book. You are indeed a person dedicated to the task of ensuring that your own impending future fate goes well. You have alleviated your loved ones of an over-whelming and daunting burden that would otherwise be facing them if you had not yourself endured the tough task of making those many challenging decisions relating to YOU. I commend you on your fortitude in accomplishing all that this book encourages you to do!

But now it is time for the next phase. You have looked death in the eye just as I did when creating this book. You have already allowed your mind to envision those mourning your passing, and you have considered all those who will suffer from your loss. You have moved through these topics mentally and emotionally. The hard stuff is done. I know it was not easy. But I now want to leave you with one last notion.

> Dying is something we human
> beings do continuously,
> not just at the end of our physical
> lives on this earth.
> ~ELISABETH KüBLER-ROSS

Every hour, every minute, every second we lose time. I encourage you to savor your precious moments and find reasons each day for smiles and laughter. And, share your happiness with those around you. Cheerfulness is so contagious! Feel the warmth of sun shining upon you and take it in. Take care of yourself and those you love. Be kind to yourself. Love yourself. Share your love with others. Make your memories and moments count!

I hope you face your life with new abandonment and incorporate exciting meaning into every single day left on this magnificent planet. You are no longer hiding behind those "what ifs" and unfinished business. You are free! You have faced the fear and made peace with it. You are now in tranquil harmony with your life and your death.

Live life with the utmost passion. Visit those people you have made many EXCUSES not to visit but not really any good REASONS. Take that trip. Look at your "Bucket List" and "KICK-the-Bucket List," and start working those items one by one. Check them off! Do not leave this wonderful place with things in front of you never to have been accomplished. Conquer them and create new goals in which to embark! You've wrangled death, so full life and full steam ahead!

We only get ONE life here, and NONE of us get out alive! SEIZE!

CHAPTER 21

Celebrate!

Yes, it's that time! Time to celebrate your accomplishments! Share your good news with your family if you wish. Tell your friends. You are an adult, or this book would not be pertinent to you so enjoy your favorite adult beverage if you wish! Kool-Aid, Jim Beam...a nice glass of wine or refreshing ice water. Whatever it is, bask in the moment of celebration and ACCOMPLISHMENT!

I am very proud of you for embarking on this journey of planning, self-reflection, and getting your final affairs in order! Your first big step was getting this book or even opening it, if it was a gift. But you took it seriously and got the job done! Continue the celebration into tomorrow, and the next day. In fact, make sure you find SOMETHING to celebrate in each and every day. This book was about dying. But, you've addressed that fate. Now, it is about LIVING!

I wish you the best in your continued and marvelous life journey. I hope this experience has allowed you to handle the various unfinished or unresolved matters that were pending and causing you concern. I hope you enjoyed this journey as much as possible. I hope you were a tiny bit entertained and encouraged in the process. Most of all, I hope an insatiable zest for sensational, meaningful, and extraordinary living has been encouraged along the way.

So, let me ask you one more time. ***Are you ready to die?*** I asked you earlier in this book, and I am fairly positive everyone responded with a resounding **"NO!"** But, now I am asking again...**Are you ready to die?** If you've completed this book, the answer is now **"YES!"** I didn't ask if you ***wanted*** to die. I asked if you were **READY**, as in **PREPARED**. And, now you most certainly are!

My hopes are that you will be well for many years, fill your days with excitement and enrichment, and have no suffering upon your passing. And, I also wish for you to have the perfect final farewell celebration that leaves people in "AWE" of the magnificent life you have lived and distinctly illuminates the wonderful and amazing person you truly are!

May you live abundantly between your Sunrises and Sunsets!

You must live in the present,
launch yourself on every wave,
find your eternity in each moment.
Fools stand on their island of opportunities
and look toward another land.
There is no other land; there is no other life but this.
~HENRY DAVID THOREAU

The End

ABOUT THE AUTHOR

Holley Kelley is passionate about latter-life planning! And it shines through in *Sunrises and Sunsets*!

She combines her expertise in the area of journalism and her professional training in the field of gerontology to help usher people through important advance-care and final-affairs planning like no other! As an entrepreneur and a Credentialed Professional Gerontologist awarded through the National Association of Professional Gerontologists, Holley has uncovered a way to make planning for tomorrow a successfully fun and lively adventure. All the while, her focus is about living your best live NOW!

Holley hosts engaging *Sunrises and Sunsets* workshops, which are full of enthusiasm and energy, and offer a supportive approach to completing her *Sunrises and Sunsets* book. These workshops appeal to book clubs, corporate groups; church, family, social, or civic groups; and any other club, organization, or group that is interested in getting their final affairs in order in a FUNdamental way. Both a value and a comprehensive approach, these workshops deliver!

Meeting for eight weeks for two hours per week, Holley leads groups through all areas of advance-care planning, as the *Sunrises and Sunsets* book is explored from beginning to end. What is promised? A lot of FUN and an unexpected adventure! These workshops are productive, pleasant and personal—social, savvy, and satisfyingly spectacular! But, most of all they are YOUR Final Affairs Forged with Flair, Finesse and FUNctionality!

Holley delights in opportunities to share her message on latter-life planning as well as learning more about beneficial community groups and organizations, through speaking engagements and important community events. She is a captivating public speaker with an engaging style, who has extensive experience in professionally addressing a vast array of groups. Her topics range from issues on aging, final-affairs planning, to subjects in the field of gerontology. One thing is certain; she is sure to keep her audiences wanting to hear more! She commands a listening presence and is lively, intelligent, witty, and an incredibly talented storyteller. Regardless of the topic, when her speech is over, you'll still be reflecting about her essential message!

Another area of Holley's focus is life's inevitable destiny—funerals. Holley's custom funeral writing and officiating is full of personal creativity, genuine depth, and they are intensely compassionate. She articulates in the most incredible detail, the decedent's life in a sincere and honorable fashion. Through her words so eloquently written, she is able to bring lives to a gentle close, while celebrating the unique life of those who have passed on. Her delivery of a eulogy is absolutely memorable, heartfelt, and emotional. Those who have heard her officiate a funeral claim her words can help people heal (even amidst challenging dynamics), and Holley remarkably inspires traces of hope and happiness during life's most sorrowful times.

Holley also serves people in her practice as a gerontologist, in which her focus is on latter-life issues and providing consulting services. She is able to convey her thoughts in ways clients both enjoy and become part of their planning experience. She is an educator. Her goal is to make sure her clients understand the topics they are discussing. Holley's approach to life and her work is professional, honest, passionate, and contagious!

Holley finds beauty in simplicity. She is deeply rooted spiritually on a personal level. She believes in life by both destiny and design, in that the wonderful opportunities that life bestows are ours to proactively define, design, and develop for our desired outcome. She is also a big advocate of gratitude! She believes in keeping our priorities balanced for a healthy and fruitful life and to continually strive towards our true purpose and highest best self.

She has been a life-long equestrian. She owns Spotted Saddle and Tennessee Walking horses and loves being in the saddle, exploring the trails in the South and riding in the mountains. She is happy living at the foothills of the Smoky Mountains where opportunities for riding are endless. She values nature and is often in awe of the beauty that abounds in the great outdoors. Holley is also fascinated with the old west and Native American cultures. In her leisure time she likes target practicing and skeet shooting. She enjoys spending time with friends and visiting relatives. She lives with her husband and two amazing children, their two dogs, a Newfoundland and Chihuahua, as well as their horses, in the beautiful Tennessee valley area of Northern Alabama. In her spare time, Holley will be working on her next book.

To learn more about Holley, or her professional endeavors, services, the book, or her workshops, please visit her at www.sunrisesandsunsetsbook.com.

Do You Want to Make it Easier for Your Loved Ones After YOUR Sunset?

Financial planners, CPA's, Attorney's, Funeral Establishments, give this to your new clients and patrons.

Give this as a corporate or convention gift.

Give this as a personal gift to your family members and friends.

Therapists and workshop leaders, support groups, assisted living and retirement communities activities directors, use this for an eight-week program or a long weekend workshop.

This is a great book to work together in a group,
such as a book club or a group of friends.
See www.sunrisesandsunsetsbook.com
for more information and access to The Leader's Guide.

To obtain more copies of *Sunrises and Sunsets*,
ask your favorite bookstore to carry it,
or go to the author's website at
www.sunrisesandsunsetsbook.com for more information,
including *Sunrises and Sunsets* book workshops!

FOR QUANTITY DISCOUNTS,
Contact the publisher directly:

Robert D. Reed Publishers
P.O. Box 1992
Bandon, Oregon 97411
www.rdrpublishers.com
E-mail: 4bobreed@msn.com
Phone: (541) 347-9882; Fax: -9883